How to become a Virtual Assistant?

Work from home with
Flexibility and Freedom

by

Julie Farmer

Revised and Republished in 2020 by myPA Virtual Services Publishing.
Copyright Julie Farmer.

Designed by Julie Farmer, Printed in the UK by myPA Virtual Services Publishing.

myPA Virtual Services Publishing
Brunel House, Volunteer Way, Faringdon, Oxfordshire, SN7 7YR
www.mypavirtualservices.com
www.juliefarmer.com
ISBN: 978-0-9571095-5-1

2

Contents

Section One
A Little about the history of a Virtual Assistant and
What service you could offer as a Virtual Assistant

Section Two
Setting up your business and what you need to consider
and plans you need to put into practice

Section Three
The practical aspects of setting up as Virtual
Assistant business and running your business

Section Four
All about the finance within your business

Section Five
Conclusion

Introduction

My name is Julie Farmer, and in 2002, I set up a Virtual Assistant in Oxfordshire, United Kingdom. It has been 18 years since I started on this adventure and I am just as passionate today as I was when I started. I now employ a few people who work with me, and we cover a range of administrative and secretarial services for a wide variety of clients.

Over the last 18 years, our world has got smaller with advances in technology. However, communication has proved the key to any successful business; it just means we now have more ways to communicate with each other. It is now commonplace to talk to somebody via your computer who lives halfway around the world, send files as email attachments, and even view and work on documents remotely.

The skills and services of a talented Virtual Assistant/PA are still in high demand as Virtual Assistant can work with anybody, anywhere, any time. This is a new way of working and an incredibly fulfilling career.

I wrote this book in 2011 and have revised it in 2020 to help and give you an insight into this ever-expanding profession and share with you some of my experiences. I aim to provide you with an idea of what it is like to be a Virtual Assistant and tell you what you need to know to start up as a Virtual Assistant yourself.

Julie

Julie Farmer
myPA Virtual Services (www.mypavirtualservices.com)

Section One

Choosing to be a Virtual Assistant

WHAT IS A VIRTUAL ASSISTANT?

Having run a successful Virtual Assistant business for nearly sixteen years, I am still asked this question. I suppose the term is not familiar to everybody and it can sound like quite a strange concept. The question is usually closely followed by "why use a Virtual Assistant" and then "I could do this myself much cheaper" This first chapter explores both the concept of the Virtual Assistant and the reasons why people and businesses choose to employ one.

I would describe a Virtual Assistant (VA) as follows: someone who works for a small business or organisation but is not directly employed by them, yet who has accountability for the work they do on their behalf. They are, in effect, a subcontractor who provides secretarial and/or administrative support.

The duties of a VA can include scheduling activities such as meetings, organising travel, social media, customer service, email campaigns, bookkeeping and much more. A VA can work from their own office (they might, for example, rent office space in a shared building), from their home office, or the offices of their clients. They can also do a combination of any of these.

The definition of a Virtual Assistant on the Wikipedia website is as follows:

"A Virtual Assistant (typically abbreviated to VA, also called a virtual office assistant) is an entrepreneur who provides professional administrative, technical, or creative (social) assistance to clients from a home office… They usually work for other small businesses, brokers and consultancy groups. The estimates are that there are as few as 5,000-8,000 or as many as

25,000 Virtual Assistants worldwide; the profession is growing in centralised economies with "fly-in, fly-out" (FIFO) staffing practices." www.wikipedia.org. I think you will find that this figure is increasing year in year out.

There is currently a debate in the industry about the title of a Virtual Assistant and whether 'we' as an industry should change it. The general feeling is that the title 'Assistant', to those who aren't familiar with the industry, doesn't give an accurate impression of the variety of roles a VA can fulfil.

I believe there are four types of Virtual Assistants:

- **Virtual Assistant (VA)** – A VA is someone who has the ability to assist their client with several secretarial and administrative tasks, generally on a short-term project basis. Equally, they may undertake specific jobs over a period of time; for example, creating a database from business cards.
- **Virtual Personal Assistant (VPA)** – A VPA is someone who works closely with a small business owner, providing secretarial and administrative support, and who is there for the long-term. The relationship is similar to that of employer and employee. However, the VPA will only visit the client once or twice a week. Despite the longevity of the relationship, the VPA is self-employed.
- **Virtual Executive Assistant (VEA)** – A VEA is someone who works closely with a small business owner to provide secretarial and administrative support. They also get involved in some of the business development for the company. The VEA is an integral part of the business, becoming one of the planners and authorising partners.
- **Personal Assistan**t – A PA is someone who generally works for one person in one organisation. However, in the VA world, many VAs call themselves PAs as many employers/clients understand this term better.

For this book, I am going to use the term 'Virtual Assistant' (VA) to include all of the above.

Why would I want to become a VA

There are many benefits to becoming a VA. One of the most exciting is that you become an entrepreneur; you are your own boss.

Let's take a look at a few of the benefits that come along with that.

Flexibility As a VA, you can decide what hours you work as well as what jobs you want to undertake. If a job sounds intriguing, great, do it. If not, you can pass and continue looking for something else. Some clients will want you to be available during precise hours, while others will want you to be more project-based. As long as you complete the project in line with the agreed specification and deadline, you can work whatever hours you want, which in turn provides an invaluable opportunity for working around the other demands of your life, such as parenting or time-consuming hobbies. A word of caution: there is flexibility in being a VA, but it has to work both ways. Your clients will often have tight deadlines to meet and adhere to. On occasion, you may have to fall in line and change your plans to help your clients' need and their 'deadlines'.

Diversity As a VA, you can work for clients in your home town, your home county, or even around the world. You can have a variety of working with one client, answering emails and scheduling speaking engagements and an hour later making sales calls for a minibus hire company. It certainly keeps things fresh and exciting. If you find you are not enjoying a job, you have the opportunity for change with the next work you take on.

Longevity You may get the opportunity to work for a client who would like you to become a long-term part of their team. They may be in the process of expanding their business and know that they have a fixed number of hours of administrative support needed each month, which can be an advantageous contract, as you truly get involved in your client's business. It is also significant from the perspective of knowing you have some element of guaranteed income each month. It is worth searching for this kind of contract. When times are hard, contracts are lost, a long-standing relationship with a trusted client will save your business.

Work Environment Many VAs love the fact that they can work from a home office, which generally means in their own home. It is very convenient for parents who also have to take care of the needs of their family. Other VAs prefer going to an office to do their work. They find that the structure of working in an office environment is much better for their productivity. In some cases, you can even work from the client's office. The choice is yours.

Pay You can set your pay scale. You decide the minimum amount you will work for, per hour or for each job. If more in-depth knowledge and skills are required, you can ask for a higher rate. You can also encourage your client to pay for additional training to complete tasks. (I have been sent on a software testing training course for one client, this has given them the skills they needed and me an extra qualification).

Most VAs operate as their own business, so you will need to keep in mind the tax implications and set your pay scale accordingly. We will talk more about the financial aspects of being a VA later in the book.

Choosing Your VA Location

As I have mentioned, you get to make your own choice regarding where you work. You can even decide to change it from time to time. Let's take a look at some of the advantages and disadvantages when you are choosing your VA location.

- Working from Home
- Working from an Office
- Working from a Client's Office

Working from an Office

Some people prefer the psychological feeling of being 'at work' while keeping a clear boundary between home and their job. It is possible to rent office space in shared buildings, along with other small business owners.

Ultimately, the decision is yours; just make sure you weigh the advantages and disadvantages of your situation. However, if you

try it one way and don't like it, you can change at a suitable point and try something else. You're in charge, remember.

My first office (picture to the left), was a rented desk and an outdated computer and a mobile phone the size of a brick. I shared the office with another small business which had started two days before I had. I have some good memories of that office and some bad. One of the tasks I undertook for this office was to clean the entire office block for free rent. It was something I did for about 12 months when I was setting up. Looking back, I am very proud of myself. At the time, I hated every minute of it.

Who Can Become a VA?

One of the beautiful things about becoming a VA is that you don't have to have a qualification, 'certificate' or specialised education. Generally, having experience in clerical and/or administrative tasks is all it takes to be a VA. We will cover more about what it takes to be a good VA – and there is a difference.

You will also need to make sure that you have the proper frame of mind to become a VA. Although the idea of flexibility sounds attractive, it does not suit everyone. Some people just work better in a more structured environment. However, if you love the entrepreneurial aspect of working when and how you want, then you can be a VA.

Services a VA Can Offer or Specialise in

There are many different services or specialities that a VA can offer. While most VA work is clerical or administrative, here are some other options you can consider:

Social Media If you are familiar with Facebook, Twitter, Foursquare, LinkedIn, TikTok, Pinterest, Instagram, blogging and other types of social media, you can offer to manage a client's social media campaigns. While a client is running a business, they can struggle to find the time to post messages on their Facebook or Twitter account or to check Foursquare. Once you get to know your client and their personality, you can post messages on their behalf, as if you are them. If they are just starting with social media, you can help them further by mapping out their entire campaign – when and what should be done on a daily or weekly basis to promote their business.

Mobile Marketing One of the newest forms of growing a business is through mobile marketing. As well as basic SMS/text messaging, mobile marketing involves a full array of marketing to mobile phones via Bluetooth, proximity systems and services linked to the web. The full range of mobile marketing is complex; however, this can be extremely effective. If you know (or are willing to learn) how it all works, you will have a fabulous service to offer your clients.

Search Engine Optimisation (SEO) –This is the nuts and bolts of growing an online business. A website is a great start, but if no one knows the website is there, it is a waste of your client's 'virtual real estate'. Knowing how to perform keyword research, submit to article directories and how to increase a client's rating on Google/LinkedIn search results is a valuable asset. All website have to be compatible with all mobile devices. Mobile devices are smartphones, table and any other device available, think about the emerging market of smartwatches?

Website Design/Management and Blogging. If you can design and create a website, this is a skill which will stand you in good stead. 'WordPress' is the 'standard' in website design and management. It is relatively easy to understand, and specific settings are free, for example, setting up a blog. However, if you want more functionality and control, there may be a small fee. If you are not familiar with it already, I suggest you go online and start to understand its functions and how you and your clients can use it. It is a secure platform to build a website on and is simple to change and manipulate. Once you know one web design platform, you can learn others more easily. Other website platforms are appearing daily, but, creating a website is a valuable service you can offer your clients. You could also link with a website developer and undertake a joint venture in website design. It's up to you and how much energy you want to put into this side of your business.

Specialised Writing If you are adept at writing, make sure to let your clients know. Many clients can use an excellent copywriter to design flyers, brochures and pamphlets. If you have experience in a specialised area such as technical writing or sales letters, be sure to offer that as well.

Internet Research If you enjoy surfing the web and research information, offer your services as an internet researcher. It is common for businesses to need some research done, but often they don't require someone to be employed long-term for this type of work. A VA is a perfect solution.

Postal Services This can be divided into two types of services. The first is the VA acting as a shipping and packing department for your client. Packing products and dealing with couriers and postal services. Small business owners need to focus on working on their business, not on the administrative details such as postal services. As a VA, you can offer a necessary service that will save them time.

The second service is to offer a postal business address; this is very lucrative. The client will pay you a monthly fee and, you deal with incoming post and deliveries. A word of warning: If a business or individual uses your address as their business address and they get a county court judgement against them, you may get the bailiffs turning up at your door. It would then be your responsibility to prove that everything in your office/home belongs to you and therefore, cannot be ceased. I have had bailiffs turning up at my office address doing this. It can be scary, but if you deal with the bailiff professionally, you can work through this.

Database Management/Creation and Reporting This is another example of a VA being able to help small business by alleviating some of the necessary but time-consuming workloads. By creating and managing a database and handing over weekly reports to the business owner, you enable your client to focus on improving their business performance. They can focus on their business instead of in it and more importantly, this will help your client with a marketing strategy and sales planning as well as creating intellectual property for your client should he or she decide to sell their business.

Typing Services – Copy and Audio. Many business owners use a small recording device to keep notes of ideas or projects. A VA can specialise in transcribing this audio copy into notes that the owner can review and put into action. I enjoy this type of service. It is a great line of work for you to get into as your client can send you reports, quotes and letters. With your client's agreement, you can take on the full lifecycle of transcribing the copy, sending the documents out and ensuring that they have reached their destination (in effect creating an extended role from just audio typing).

It is interesting to note that transcription software is now available, but this service is still popular.

Bookkeeping This is another common specialisation of VAs. Many businesses don't need or employ a full-time bookkeeper. As a VA, you can offer bookkeeping of several different businesses during the month. You will need to understand accounting terms, the legal ramifications of company formations, regulations and tax liabilities. If this is a service you enjoy, then undertaking some formal qualifications would be very useful. As a VA, you should only offer basic bookkeeping skills, dealing with expenses, creating invoices. Bookkeeping in-depth will require qualifications.

Ethics of a VA

It is important to note that as you are working with a wide variety of clients, you will learn a vast amount of information about their company. You may work for a client that is a direct competitor of somebody you have worked for in the past, or currently work for. It is essential that you follow a strict code of ethics and never divulge one company's information to another, even if you think it could help them or 'may not hurt' the other company. Many companies will ask you to sign a Non-Disclosure Agreement (NDA) before working for them. In basic terms, this means that you agree not to share ANY information about their company with any other. Take this seriously. Even if you aren't required to sign an NDA, it is always advisable to have your own.

Dress code One of the things that many VAs enjoy about being their own boss is that they can work from home, which in turn means wearing whatever they want. This could mean the joy of working in pyjamas or not having to wear make-up. My personal experience is that VAs who work from home, still get up and get ready for work by putting on clean clothes and doing their hair; they feel and act more professional throughout the day. You don't have to wear a suit, but at least put something on that you wouldn't be embarrassed to answer the door in or attend a meeting.

When visiting a client, you must ensure you are dressed appropriately. If the usual rule of thumb is that your client wears a suit and their staff are dressed in appropriate attire, then you must follow suit. It would not be appropriate to turn up wearing jeans and a T-shirt when other members of staff are all wearing suits.

Regarding working from an office environment, I'd like to share a story with you:

> When I began my business, and before I had any clients, I made the decision, I wanted to get my business structure, ethos and internal procedures organised. I gave little thought to my outward appearance, and I would arrive at the office in jeans and a T-shirt or jumper, and trainers. I wanted to be comfortable, but I soon realised how crucial first impressions are - no matter what you are doing. I was pulled aside by another business owner, with whom I was sharing an office. She carefully mentioned that comments had been made regarding my appearance and that I always looked a bit disorganised. The clothes I was wearing were not office attire. She suggested that as I was selling office services, I should dress appropriately. I had not considered this point until then as I was still in the planning stages, although I had already exhibited in Oxfordshire. I knew my fellow office tenants

and understood they only wanted the best for me and my business. I took the comments on board, and to this day, I still get feedback from them on the clothes that I wear.

I am more aware of the impression my attire can give potential clients so always dress accordingly. I am telling you this as it is important to note that even after years of running my business and having built up a reputation based on the quality of my work, people will still make decisions based on their initial appraisal of me. My image is a part of this. Remember that a person's first impression will be imprinted in their mind. Decide what you want that impression to be.

Verbal language If you are working from home, don't get lazy. Make sure you are using language correctly, and not falling into the habits of using slang. If you are working over the phone, it is important that you practice sharp enunciation, especially if you are working with clients in another country.

Also, practice having a 'smile' in your voice. You will be amazed at how much of an impression this can make on your clients. They want someone professional, cheerful and enthusiastic, especially if they are expecting you to represent them while interacting with their clients.

Body language You may think it sounds silly, but your body language can be 'heard' over the phone. Sit up straight, and your professionalism will shine through. If you are in an office, body language becomes even more critical. Remember my story about first impressions. If someone 'sees' you rolling your eyes when you are talking on the phone, the impression will be that you don't care.

The bottom line is, no matter where you are working – at home, at an office or your client's office, keep an ethical and professional manner at all times.

Why Clients Use A VA

The most common reasons a client will be looking for a VA to work with them are:

Non-core business needs Small business owners want to concentrate on the core of their business – for example, a freelance surveyor will want to be carrying out surveys and meeting potential new clients. To have somebody to take on the more day-to-day aspects of their business, or areas which they are not experienced in, allows them to concentrate on what they do best.

Resources A small business does not have the need or resources for a permanent administrator or secretarial role, so using a VA enables them to employ someone for ad hoc projects, or regular tasks, as and when they are required.

Skill-based There may be an ad hoc requirement for a specialised service such as creating a CRM system, and your client does not have the skill or resource within their business to complete the project.

Convenience and time-saving Having a service which is accessible within a short timescale, and often performed by somebody who you already know (and who already knows your business) is extremely convenient and saves a client the time of having to source and train a part-time, temporary, or even casual employee. It also saves on the associated red tape which comes with recruiting somebody to join a business. These benefits should not be underestimated.

They do not want to do the task themselves. Sometimes people have an aversion to certain types of work. If you have a client who hates administrative tasks such as letter merges, postal campaigns, then you need to let them know how easy it would be for you to do it all on their behalf. If it gets them out of a task they hate and frees up their time to do something they want to do; they will realise your value.

Not spending enough time with their family This is a common problem for small business owners, as businesses are time-consuming, and many people are so passionate about what they do that their family time can get eroded without them even realising it. Using a VA for specific tasks can alleviate some of the pressure and workload and enable clients to create more of a balance between these two essential areas of their life.

Outsourcing is cost-effective. A VA is easier than recruiting a new member of staff, and the client will not have to comply with employment law. They will not have to worry about sick pay, about holiday pay or cover. They will not worry about finding extra space in their office, buying additional computer equipment or licences. There will also be no need to provide for Pension cover or Healthcare costs.

Other tasks taking their time Up Sometimes there simply is not enough time in the day to undertake all the tasks a business needs to cover, in which case a VA is once more invaluable, as their services can be employed for specific aspects of a job – or for keeping the day-to-day business going –for a client to complete an important project.

What a Client will be Looking For in a VA

Although as a VA, a client will not expect you to go through the same application process as if you were applying for a job as their direct employee, they will still want to vet you and be sure of your skills, reliability, professionalism and so on.

A good idea is to have some testimonials/references available from previous clients. If this is difficult because you are just starting up, try to obtain references from former employers, and a personal recommendation from a professional acquaintance. The attributes which a potential client could be looking for are:

Professionalism Illustrate this through personal appearance, language and well-presented business literature. Although you work for yourself, you still need to be someone that other people would want working for them.

Personality Potential clients will want to know they can work with you, so try to strike a balance of friendly and formal; without being too formal. You need to be approachable.

Skills/experience/qualifications You should always provide a copy of your CV which will show your roles before becoming a VA as well as examples of work undertaken since setting up on your own. Offer copies of certificates where appropriate.

Reliability If you say you will call a client at a particular time, be prompt. Respond to their emails within a given timeframe. References from other clients would also be useful here.

Communication Overlapping all aspects of how you conduct your business; effective communication is essential when presenting yourself to potential clients. You need to ensure your client is confident of your communication skills, whether face-to-face, in writing or just generally throughout jobs. Offer regular updates (not too often – you can agree on the timings with the client based on a particular job) so that they know you are still there, and still working for them as the job or project progresses.

Honesty This is hugely important and will only really become apparent once you are working for someone. From the outset, you need to be honest about the length of time that you think a job will take and any costs involved. Again, testimonials/references would be useful to vouch for you, but it can also be fairly easy to spot if someone is not completely honest. There is no point in 'stretching the truth' to get work. You will feel stressed, you will be found out, and you will create a bad reputation for yourself.

The key thing a client is looking for in a VA is somebody to ease their workload and their mind. You need to create confidence in a client, so they can let you get on with the work required. They need to get on with their job, without having to watch over you or keep chasing you for updates.

If you can present the right initial impression and then carry out the job(s) required as promised, you will begin to build a healthy and fruitful relationship which will benefit both you and your client.

Section Two

Business Basics

Business Basics

When you are starting up a business, it can be challenging to know where to begin and how to make the transition from employee to self-employed.

The most important thing is to make a plan. The saying 'fail to plan, plan to fail' is undoubtedly true, so first set aside some time to decide precisely what it is you want to do in your business before you even begin to think about how you are going to do it.

The planning and early stages of your VA business are vital to its eventual success. It is essential that you create some solid foundations for your business. You will need to know what you want to achieve, what services you want to offer and what goals you have at the beginning of your business venture, to ensure you have a much higher chance of success.

To save you sleepless nights and any financial losses due to misdirection or poor planning, we are going to focus on a few of the essential topics that you should think about when setting up your business:

- Starting Up
- Setting your Business Goals
- Organisational Skills
- Communication Skills
- Time Management Skills

Starting Up

When you start your VA business, your primary concern will always be how many clients you can get, how much you can charge them and what services you can offer.

However, before you go down that route, I would like you to stop, take a deep breath and realise that you are starting a business and your first client is your own business. I know this may sound a bit strange, but if your business does not run efficiently, legally and without effort, what kind of service are you going to be able to offer your clients?

What will the legal status of your business be? Are you going to set up as a Sole Trader, a Limited Liability Company, a Partnership or a Limited Liability Partnership? What kind of accounts are you going to be running: accrual accounting or cash accounting? Are you going to be VAT registered? Where is your VA business going to be 'officially' located; at your accountant's office?

These are all critical questions that need to be answered, and I would recommend that you spend some time thinking about this side of your business. Please don't look at all this and get nervous; it's not as hard as you may think. Once you have made a decision, stick with it, move on, and start planning.

We have already covered a little about the benefits of the different work locations, in Section One (Choosing to be a Virtual Assistant). Now it is time to decide where you want to be working each day. We will look at a couple of real-life examples which may help you in making this decision.

Choosing your Business Name

There are two learning points when choosing your business name. You need to ensure that the domain name (for your website) is available. If you have a great business name and the domain name is available, buy it immediately and don't let it go – even if you think that it may be a while before your business is up-and-running.

I had always had the idea of starting my own business, and back in 1998 I came up with the concept of 'myPA', but I didn't act on this idea for another four years. However, I did purchase the domain name of www.mypa.co.uk. I was not trading at the time and was in full-time employment. I let this domain name go, thinking that no one else would want it and that I would be able to purchase it again at a later date. Unfortunately, someone else now has this domain name, and I can never use it. As a result, I now trade under the name of myPA Business Limited and myPA Virtual Services. All my stationery is headed 'myPA Business Limited' or 'myPA Virtual Services', and I kick myself every time I think about letting my original domain name go!

The second key point is to choose a simple name that is easy to spell. As I set one of my businesses up as 'myPA Business Limited' with a domain name of www.mypabusiness.com, it means that all my email addresses are something@mypabusiness.com. I like my business name as it tells everyone what I do but putting the word 'business' in the domain name has proved to be extremely frustrating at times as it is easy to mistype. I have had quite a few situations where clients and salespeople have sent me emails which have not been received because they have spelt the word 'business' incorrectly when typing my email address, this is not to say that they can't spell the word, but when you start to type at a fast pace it is easy to transpose the letters 'i' and 'n' so the email address becomes something@mypabusniess.com.

The result is that some emails will be lost in the ether – which leads me to another learning point; it is often useful to check via telephone that an important email has been received if you have not had a reply to it. Alternatively, set a process in place with your clients to send acknowledgement emails within a set period (e.g. one working day) so that you are always confident that work and work requests/updates are received.

People know my business as 'myPA'. My clients get a great deal of satisfaction when on the phone talking to their client about how 'my PA will take care of that' (I also have a little smile about it). I won't change my company name, but I have, however, found out that 'myPA' is also a name used as a Finnish football club based in Anjalankoski founded in 1947, as well as a perfume. There are also other VAs using myPA in their name.

Where will you Work?

Working from Home: Janet started working from home in early 2010. She had been hired to do some temporary collection/credit control work for a company. This required her to be on the telephone for around eight hours a day while sitting in front of a computer. She needed a quiet place so that she could make calls and concentrate on her workload.

She set her office up in an area of her home where she could be separated from her family when they were home. Her husband moved the TV and the games console downstairs so that her children would still have access to them. It seemed like the perfect scenario. The children would go to school during the day; her husband would go out to work so that Janet could work at home undisturbed all day.

It wasn't that easy.

Here are some of the obstacles she faced in the first few weeks that she didn't anticipate:

* Children off ill from school
* No-school days
* Children arguing
* Husband and children wondering why dinner was not made when they got home from school and work
* Husband and children used to having access to Janet 24 hours a day, seven days a week
* Friends stopping by during the day, not understanding that Janet needed to be upstairs working
   * No one to discuss work issues or problems with
   * No one to celebrate success with

One of the first things you need to understand about working from home is that you are doing just that working from home. You need to be very strict with yourself, your partner, your children and your friends, especially in the beginning. When you are 'at Work', your time belongs to your clients. If you stop to have a chat with your friend who 'just popped in' to have a coffee, then you are no longer working for your client, and you have lost valuable billing time in your business. Think of it like this: if you are working for your client and you are charging £25 per hour, your 30 minutes chat with your friend has cost you £12.50 (plus the coffee).

When you have scheduled time for your client, you need to focus 100 per cent on the tasks you are performing for them. This means you are not taking a break to throw in a load of laundry or quickly unload the dishwasher. You are not making dinner preparations. You are not vacuuming up dog hair. You are working for your clients. Which means you can bill them for your time, which is how you are going to earn money. You are not setting up your business for the fun of it; you have financial obligations that need to be met, and you have chosen the VA route to meet these obligations. Time really is money, and it is money that gives you time.

Janet finally had to sit her husband and children down and say, "I am working from 7 am – 3 pm every day. I am not able to do laundry, make dinner, clean or run your forgotten homework to school during that time. You need to imagine that I am working at an official office, and your expectations of me need to change."

She also needed to ignore her phone unless it was a client or her children's school. If she had been at the office, she would not have known her home phone was ringing. In the same way, unless she was taking a break or having lunch, she did not answer the phone for non-essential calls. (A good tip here is to use the 'caller display' service on your phone, or even to have a separate phone for work.)

The sooner your family and friends realise how 'working from home' actually works, the easier it will be for you.

What can we learn from Janet about setting up your home workspace and schedule?

1   You must have a location that can be separate from the rest of your family. Of course, a designated room would work the best, but that is not always possible. Have a desk or workspace, where you can have some degree of a noise barrier from the rest of the goings-on in your home.

2   Your family must respect that when you are in your workspace, you are off-limits, except in an emergency. On the days that Janet's family were at home, the children needed to learn that they should go to Dad too for their disagreements and questions. It took some transition time, but they soon discovered that Mum was not the only one with answers or who could sort out any issues that had arisen.
3   You must also have a set schedule. In the beginning, Janet's schedule was working for four hours, taking a one-hour break at lunch to get some things done around the house, and then another four hours. Scheduling allowed her to keep on top of things around the house: laundry, dinner, cleaning, dishes, etc. Having that time in the middle of the day allowed her to focus on her clients' work during the remaining work hours.
4   Your schedule does not necessarily have to be during daytime hours. Maybe you are a night owl, and the best time for you to concentrate and get things done is at night. You are in control of your schedule, so work when you work best. However, remember that you must have a time each day to work with your clients. Even if you decide to work from 8 pm to 4 am, you need to make yourself available at some point during the day for client contact; as it is likely, they will prefer more standard hours.

Working from home – advantages

- Save petrol and lunch money
- Save on buying' work clothes.'
- Get some housework done during the day
- Get the kids off for school – and be home when they get home
- No co-workers to distract you by chatting
- Working from home – disadvantages
- Easily distracted by household work
- Easily distracted by the TV
- Sometimes harder to stay focused
- Can feel less like 'Work' – and that feeling can come across to clients

- Feelings of isolation - no colleagues to interact with and email/instant messenger communications are just not quite the same as the 'real thing.'

Working from an Office If you decide to rent office space for your business, many of the problems Janet encountered will not apply to your situation. You may, however, have other issues.

You may not have as much flexibility in your hours, especially if your family needs you at home during the evenings. You would possibly need to have more of a typical 9-5 schedule. You would not have the advantage of 'working around' a sick child, where you could juggle working and caring for a sick child if you were at home.

Another VA I know decided she was going to work from an office. Mary felt as though she didn't have space at home to work effectively. She found an office to rent and enjoyed being able to get out of the house and away from its distractions and imagined it would be the best of both worlds. She could concentrate on her work, yet be available to pick the children up from school or stay at home if needed.

Mary set time for her work schedule and thought everything would follow smoothly on from there.

Just as Janet faced unexpected challenges, so too did Mary. The first time one of Mary's boys was sick and needed to stay at home from school, Mary realised that all of her work projects were at her office. She was simply going to have to go in. She decided to take her son with her and let him play a hand-held video game while she worked. What Mary failed to think about was how this would work when she was on the phone. As clients called in, Mary's son was asking her questions, and when she couldn't answer, he got frustrated and started crying. The clients at the other end of the phone could hear what was going on, and it did not come across as very professional.

The other challenges that Mary didn't expect were the extra expenses involved in running an office. She couldn't just show up to work in a tracksuit. As with my example in Section One, Mary found that she had to take the time to create the right external impression. Even though she was working for herself, she still needed to make an effort with her appearance.

Mary also found that it was too easy to work 'just a little longer' at the office, and by the time she got home, she found she was too tired and didn't have the energy to make dinner or play with the kids. She learned that she had to be just as strict with her hours at the office as Janet had to be at home. Allowing herself to become too sucked into her business may have been productive for achieving work-related goals and generating income, but it wasn't as productive to her family or social life.

Working from an office home – advantages

- The feeling of going to a 'real job.'
- Easier to stay focused
- Nice to have a real address when giving out business cards
- More comfortable to have potential clients to visit – professional appearance
- Interaction with other business owners
- Support, help and guidance may be available from fellow tenants
- Social element, meaning that you do not feel so isolated

Working from an office home – disadvantages

- Travel costs
- Travel time
- Cost of buying lunch (though you could always bring lunch from home)
- Not so family-friendly
- Costs for renting office space

Working from a Client's Office

There are times when it is going to be advantageous to work from your client's office, and this can be a very enjoyable experience. You are not interrupted by the telephone and can concentrate entirely on your client and his or her needs. I work from a number of my clients' offices and, I always need to ensure that I take several thick jumpers and trousers that don't show the dirt since I know that I will have one or two dogs jumping on me or that I have to walk through a farmyard to get to the office.

Some people like to feel part of the place they are working in, and what better way than to be on your client's site?

Working from a client's office – advantages

- Quickly develop your understanding of the company you are working for
- Familiarity with office procedures
- Easy access to required materials
- Professional atmosphere
- The client covers overhead costs
- Your client can feel more confident in giving you even more work and responsibility

Working from a client's office – disadvantages

- Office politics
- Possibility to get pulled into jobs that aren't part of your agreement
- Travel costs
- Travel time
- Harder to stay focused when other people can provide distractions
- Not so family-friendly

Whichever option you choose, remember to realise all the costs involved; not just financial.

Balance is important in all things.

Setting your Business Goals

How do I become a successful businessperson and the person I dream of being?

As explored in the first section of this book, a VA can work in several different ways, with several different specialities. Think about what appeals to you, and what you know you are good at and you enjoy. From this starting point, you can see what you want to achieve. Goals will help provide structure to your business.

A goal is defined as the purpose toward which an endeavour is directed; an objective http://www.thefreedictionary.com

The best way to become the successful business person you dream of being is to set yourself goals and ensure that you stay focused on them.

If you are the kind of person who has lots of ideas, it is easy to be pulled into something else and to go off on a tangent, and if you try to do too much at once, you will struggle. You are likely to lose sight of your original aims, and further down the line, you will wonder where you are and how you got there but more importantly, why have you not achieved your original goals.

This does not mean that you have to disregard new ideas, but once you have started turning your plan into reality, it is better to keep yourself on track. The simple approach is to keep a record of other ideas which occur to you, so you can return to them once you have achieved your original goals.

When I first started myPA, I didn't have a structured business plan or any specific goals, for the first six to eight months. My plan was simply to set up my business, get my company name known locally, and just start working. As far as I was concerned, I knew what I wanted to do and how I wanted to do it. I wanted to offer concierge and business support to wealthy people who had little time or no inclination to undertake their domestic paperwork; also, I wanted to help small businesses that did not have the resources to conduct administrative and secretarial work in-house. I knew that the service I was offering would be invaluable to each potential client – surely they would automatically see this and how important I could be to their lives and/or businesses.

As time went on, I was slightly surprised to find that people didn't want concierge services. They did, however, want business support in the form of administrative and secretarial support. I got a few business support clients, and I was on my way.

As I mentioned earlier, I rented a desk in an office which I shared with another businesswoman. I soon realised that the lady I shared my office with seemed to be having far more success than I had. She was achieving better results, better standards, and better business contracts. I knew that there must be something different in her approach. On a particularly auspicious day for her, I asked her how she was managing to do so well. After a very short conversation, it transpired that she was setting herself and her business goals. At the time, it seemed to be such a small thing, but the result was a big difference between our businesses.

At the end of every week, my office partner sat down and reviewed what she had done over the last five days, and what she needed to do in the following week. This enabled her to plan her time and see clearly what she needed to do. She also had a long-term marketing plan for how she wanted her business to progress. Over the following five years, she had planned to take her business from nothing to being a successful enterprise, with the possibility of selling it on.

The difference between where she and I were, at that point, was that she had taken the time to sit and think about the broader view. She started her business knowing what she wanted as an end result, while I started my business, not knowing or planning. I soon realised that if I wanted a successful business, I should follow her lead.

I decided to create a sales and marketing plan for myPA so that I could work out whom I should target as potential clients. I thought about who my ideal client would be, then worked out my target sectors and also what figures I wanted to achieve within a given timeframe. I broke my plan down into quarters and years. I printed this report out and kept it by my desk at all times. I also made sure that I read it at the beginning and end of every week, as a way of keeping myself focused on the greater scheme of things.

It is undoubtedly easy to get carried away with finer details during a busy working week and find yourself distracted by the stresses of particular jobs. Having this report at hand was an effective and simple way of reminding me that there was a greater goal.

When I broke down my overall plan, my first goal was to get clients that would help me achieve a turnover of circa £21,000 in my first year. Within three months, I had achieved that goal. I managed to find a client worth £14,000 a year to me, and they only required me to work for 15 hours a week. The beauty of this particular client was that they also wanted me to work in the evenings and on weekends as well as during the working week, which freed up many business hours to work for other clients. This enabled me to find four other clients who, between them, took me to over my goal of £21,000.

Having set this initial goal, I discovered that this was the best way of focusing my mind and providing me with some very valuable direction.

When you're starting your business, please take my advice. Spend at least a day writing your goals. Commit to paper what you want to achieve, how you want to achieve it, and by when. If you find it difficult to do in one day, then give yourself a couple of days to work it out. On the first day, write down some goals that you would like to achieve – even if you think they seem too difficult. Put your list away and take a break from it all. Come back to it a day or two later, and you might surprise yourself. Look at your list again and think about each of the goals. Having had a bit of time away, you may be able to see things more clearly and start to see ways in which you can turn these goals into reality. Try not to think of reasons why they can't be achieved – think instead of how they can.

One way of doing this is to break things down where possible. For example, you may have decided that you want to earn £20,000 in your first year. From a starting point of zero, this seems a huge leap. However, if you break it down to twelve separate months, you are looking at the smaller amount of £1,666.67. This is still no mean feat, but by taking things one step at a time, it should look less scary and be more manageable.

This may all sound well and good on paper, but it really does work. This is not to say that things always go according to plan. There will always be situations that crop up that can throw you, but don't let these put you off. At least when you have goals, you know where you need to get to, and if something unexpected occurs, you just need to remember what your aim is. You can find another way to get there. Having a willingness to be flexible will definitely help you. If something goes wrong, don't give up. Don't feel like a failure. Just know that you can find another way. You will become a successful business person that you dream of being.

Growing your Goals with your Business

As your business grows, you will almost certainly need to revise your goals. Remember that they are part of a developing and growing concern and be ready to develop your ideas.

As you achieve one goal, make it a priority to set another. This will stop you from standing still and give you another area of focus.

It is important that you continue to commit your goals to paper so that you have them close by as a ready reminder of your overall plan.

It is also a good idea to tell the people close to you that you have set your goals, and what they are. This way, they will understand what you want to do, and also how committed you are to achieve it. Hopefully, they will support you and know that they may also need to be flexible from time to time to help you succeed.

Here are six tips for setting and achieving goals:

Identify Your Goals Write each goal down clearly. State exactly what you want to achieve, including specific details. Make sure that you include a time limit for every goal. For example:

- Sales of £20,000 for my first year – give a date
- Setting up a website for my business by end of Month Two (list a date)

At first glance, these goals may look difficult to achieve and possibly off-putting. However, if you follow the steps below you will see how they can and will be achieved.

Identify Your Obstacles By looking ahead to see what difficulties you might encounter; you will be in a better position to overcome them. Is space in your home an issue in terms of setting up an office? If this is the case, you could look at renting some office space. However, there will be cost involved with this, and you should recognise that it could have an effect on to your monthly income. So, taking the example of earning £20,000 per year (or £1,666.67 per month), how much of this would you then have to pay out in rent? By identifying this in advance, you can add to your plan to take the extra costs into account. It may mean you have to increase the amount you are looking to earn, but by recognising this in advance, you can add it to your plan, so it does not come as a nasty surprise further down the line.

Identify Contacts Nobody can do everything by themselves, and it is inevitable that at times you will need support from others. You may want to ask for some advice, or you may want to pay somebody for their professional services. When you are planning your goals, try to work out where you may need extra help.

Using the example of creating your website, you may not want to go to the bother of learning how to create one yourself. Therefore, you will need to identify someone who can help you achieve that goal. To ensure that you have an informed choice, contact three web developers and interview them – make sure that they can explain clearly what they will do, and that they are listening to what you want. Look at examples of the websites they have created in the past. Call some of their clients to get a reference/testimonial from them. Best of all would be if you can get a recommendation from somebody that you know and trust – although it is still advisable to contact two other suppliers to make sure you are happy with your choice.

Recognise your Skills Make a list of the skills and knowledge you need in order to achieve your goal. Do you have the required skills now or do you need to develop in some areas? If you are used to being an employee for somebody else, the chances are that you concentrated largely on one area of expertise and that there are aspects of running a business that you never had to bother with before.

To return to the example of setting up a website; unless it is an area you are familiar with, it may require you to develop further skills. Researching the types of websites that are competing against you or have a higher ranking than yours might be new to you. Remember that your training and education is never over; you will always be learning or doing something new. Setting up a business means that you never stop learning.

Action Plan You know what your goal is when you want to achieve it as well as who and what can help you do so. Now it's time to be specific and write out the steps for each of your goals. Assign milestone dates to each of the action steps. This becomes your action plan.

With the two goals identified earlier, you could make a detailed plan for each.

- Sales of £20,000 for my first year

As mentioned previously, £20,000 can be broken down to twelve smaller amounts of £1,666.67. An easy sum to do, but how do you go about actually earn this amount? Think about your clients, prospective or existing. What are their business needs? Is it possible that you could offer them a 'package' which would guarantee you a set number of hours work a month, for example, ten hours of secretarial support for £250? If you find seven clients who would all like to use this service, then you have found yourself a regular income of £1750 each month.

This would equate to 70 hours of secretarial support. There are, on average, 173 working hours in the month. You have only used 70 of them in this sales goal example.

You now need to make an action plan to devise exactly what the monthly package will entail. You need a list of prospective clients. You need to plan what approach you will take and what you will say. Decide when you will complete each of these steps. You now know your goal, its deadline, and all the steps in between.

- Setting up a website for my business by end of Month Two

The website example is a little different, and achieving this goal depends on how confident you would be setting up your own website – or whether you would like somebody else to do this for you. Putting a plan in place will help with this as well; breaking down what will need to happen in order to have your website up and running. If you choose to use a supplier for this, they should take care of the majority of the planning. You still need to research your options, however, and choose the right supplier, so you will still need to have a plan in place.

Once you have your supplier, they will tell you what they need from you. If you decide to do it yourself, then your plan needs to be more detailed, and you need to understand exactly what a website entails, e.g. hosting and using interactive aspects such as forms.

You will need to decide what domain name you want and find out whether it is already in use. You also need to decide on content. Write down everything that you need to do for your website, and you will see that you can achieve it all, step by step.

Take action every day. Every step is one step closer to your goal. Print your action plan out and place it where you will see it every single day. Every day ask yourself, "What am I going to do today that will get me closer to my goal?"

When you have a decision to make as to how to spend your time, ask yourself, "Is this getting me closer to my goal?"

Celebrate Achievements When you have reached a goal, take the time to celebrate your success. This will make you take a step back and feel proud of yourself – and confident that you can go on. Now you can replace your completed goal with a new one.

Positive Attitude

It may seem all well and good, writing about goals and achievements. Breaking down £20,000 to twelve smaller amounts. However, until you get out there and do it, it will still seem like a daunting challenge. It may sound like a cliché, but attitude will also be instrumental in deciding whether you achieve your goals or not.

It is essential that, no matter how you feel, that you are perceived as having a good, strong and positive attitude. If you are a positive person, this should shine through. However, all of us have off days. It is just important not to let on to clients when this is the case.

There are some things you can do to help you have a good attitude.

Surround yourself with positive people Align yourself with other new business owners who want to grow their business.

Read and listen to positive books and tapes Find CDs and music that put you in a good frame of mind. If a particular speaker gets you fired up and feeling positive, listen to them while you are driving or doing your errands.

Believe in yourself and believe in what you can do Tell yourself, "I can achieve this. I will achieve this. This is easy."

Don't listen to others who tell you it can't be done There is no room for the negative thinking and opinions of others.

Don't procrastinate Whatever you want to achieve, don't give yourself time to talk yourself out of it. Think positive and start it today.

Organisational Skills

Organisational skills are key for any VA. Not only are they important for your business, they are important for your clients as well.

When juggling a number of clients and jobs at any one time, organisational skills are what will either make or break you. Once you get into a routine, it should start to feel more natural, but at first, it may appear to be an uphill struggle.

Here are some words of advice on how to let organisational skills help you make your business a success.

Organising Your Day

Each day look at your diary/client task list. I am a proponent of organising your day the night before. By doing this and' sleeping on it', I believe you help your mind wake up the following day ready to concentrate on the tasks at hand. You will also be amazed at the ideas that will come to you.

As you start your day, take another look at the tasks you have to do for your clients. Ensure that you are allowing enough time to accomplish each of the tasks and meet their deadlines.

You also need to be sure that you schedule in time each and every day to work on your business. When your business is young, and you are developing clients, more time will need to be spent doing this. You will need to schedule marketing time (for example, getting brochures printed), networking time (such as attending events to let people know about you) and accounting time (billing your clients and making sure your records are up-to-date).

Even as your business grows, and you find yourself with more and more tasks to accomplish for clients, it is vital that you still schedule in time each day to work on your business. You will always need to spend time on marketing and networking so that your business will continue to grow and prosper.

Organising Your Workspace

Even the most organised person can become bogged down with papers, sticky notes, file folders and supplies. An organised workspace is essential to the success of your VA business, and it will save you time and money. The end result is a much better service that you can offer to your clients (not to mention a less stressful time for you). No matter what you decide to specialise in, it should always be your first priority to ensure that you offer an excellent service to your clients, as it is they who will pay your bills and recommend you to their colleagues and friends.

Think about your perfect workspace? What do you need at your fingertips? What would you use each and every day? What could you have in another location, because you rarely need it?

Here are some suggestions for setting up your office space. Some of these sound very simplistic, but they are necessary.

Spiral notebook(s) I find that a separate spiral notebook kept by my phone is invaluable. I like to make notes when I am talking to clients and find that if they are on separate pieces of paper or sticky notes, they could potentially get lost.

Filing Cabinet With all the electronic advances of today, it may seem that a filing cabinet is no longer necessary. I would recommend, however, that you have one, even if it is a small one. You are going to need to store your clients' contracts, your NDA and any tasks or research you have undertaken for your client.

White Board or Bulletin Board If you are a visual person, this is a must. Hang a whiteboard or a bulletin board where you can easily view, write and post reminders on it. You can write your priorities for the day, client requests or tasks that are urgent for your client.

Calendar One calendar, where you will include all of your daily activities, not just those relating to your business. If you have projects due on certain dates, write them on your calendar. Any client meetings need to be listed. Do you speak at a certain time each day with clients? Write it down. You do not want to miss any deadlines or important contacts with your clients.

Computer Depending on how mobile you wish to be, a laptop may be your best choice if you need to purchase a computer. This way, you can take it with you as you meet with clients.

Printer If you are purchasing a new printer, you may want to decide whether it would be more economical to go with a black-and-white laser printer instead of an ink jet colour printer. You will need to think about the needs of your own business and the needs of your clients as you make this decision.

Labels and label-maker It is always good to have labels of different sizes on hand, whether they are used for a mailer or just to label folders. A label maker will come in handy as well.

Office Supplies Don't forget standard office supplies like a stapler, tape, paper clips, envelopes, correction fluid, scissors, sticky notes, calculator, for example.

Try to make time each week to review your workspace and get rid of, or tidy away, any clutter or junk. It is very easy to let this aspect of working life slip when you are busy carrying out client work, but I am a firm believer that working in a tidy and clear environment keeps your mind clear and focused too.

36

Organising Client Contact

Whether you are making a client visit or making an important call, make sure you are organised before you do so. A good idea is to plan out what you want to say and keep some notes at hand to make sure you don't forget anything.

If you are attending a client's site, take the paperwork that you need with you and organise it in a folder before you go. This way you will be able to lay your hands on it immediately as it is required, which will be a practical demonstration of your excellent organisational skills and will reassure your client that they can be confident letting you take on some of their workload. This will also ensure that you are unlikely to lose it or forget to do any task that has been asked of you. Your organisational skills reflect the fact that you should be good at keeping to deadlines.

Communication Skills

Excellent communication skills are an absolute must for your VA business. Because you are working with people virtually, you might not have the ability to talk or work with your clients in person on a regular basis, if at all. Therefore, you are relying on your correct understanding of exactly what your client is asking you to do electronically.

You need to set expectations with regards to communication from the start. How often will you talk? What if your client needs to talk to you outside your set working hours? What is the best way for the two of you to contact each other?

It is imperative that you set aside enough time to discuss any projects you are working on and any issues or successes you hare having. Miscommunication will cause your client to lose trust in your effectiveness, and it will waste time and money.

If at all possible, talk to your client every week. This does not have to be a phone call. An email/instant messenger or a Skype conversation can be just as effective. You may not be able to charge for your chat with your client so make sure you are precise, professional and cut the call short (politely) if your client starts to tell you about what they watched on TV last night. Remember, time is money, and every time you talk to a client that you cannot bill, it is money out of your pocket. Having said that, you do need to maintain good relationships with clients, so it doesn't hurt to allow a short amount of general chat from time to time.

If you are on instant messenger, Skype or email, keep these messages to refer back to as needed. It is vitally important that you take note of each conversation. You may have agreed to do some tasks for your client and want to confirm details of them. It may be worth summarising them in a letter or email to reconfirm your discussion, especially if your client has asked you to do some additional work that will need to be billed. I know you may have a wonderful relationship with your client but when money comes into the equation, friendship will quickly disappear, and you will become a subcontractor that can easily be dismissed.

Ask questions. When you have your client's attention, ask, ask and ask some more. You want as much information as possible, so you can complete the work as your client wishes, and in a timely manner. After your conversation with them is over, you may not have another chance to raise questions again.

There are some unrealistic expectations of VAs which can be due to the client's unreasonable demands. Make sure your client understands how you work, what type of work you are able to undertake and the timescales you are prepared to work towards and ensure they suit both of you. I have heard and read of some clients expecting a VA to get work completed within an hour and yet it would take them a day to complete. Yes, a VA is good at what they do, but if you are going to research a project for a client set your boundaries from the beginning. Ask your client what time they would like the work completed by and how they would like the work reported back to them. Use reflective listening skills when receiving a task from your client. Repeat back everything they have asked you to undertake.

For example:

Client: Look online and get me a list of motorbike shops in London

VA: OK, I will look online for motorbike shops in London, how many shops do want and is this within the M25 only?

Getting the information from your client is a skill and will ultimately save you time and effort.

Time Management Skills

Your time management can absolutely make or break your business. It can also be the difference between you feeling the freedom of being a business owner or feeling like your business is a burden which is just pulling you down.

The first step in time management is working out how much time you can and want to devote to your business each week. Can you work every day? Do you prefer to work several long days and have time off in between? How much time can you spend on building your business each day? How will your work fit into your family's schedule?

Will you spend Mondays and Wednesdays working with Client A, Tuesdays and Thursdays with Client B and Fridays with Client C? Or will you work a certain number of hours for each of them each day?

Daily, you need to focus on your top priorities. Do you have a big project for one client that has a tight timeframe? Are you able to bump some other work into the next day so that you can focus on them? If you work 12 hours one day to complete a task for one client, are you able to shift the workload of your other clients to adjust for that?

As you find a schedule that works for you (usually through trial and error), your business and your family, you will begin to feel the freedom of being a business owner with good time management skills. You will control your business and your time instead of them controlling you.

Once you have gotten the hang of these skills, you will feel more confident with what you and your business are all about and will be able to watch your business grow and flourish. What is more, you will start to enjoy it.

Using an Avatar

If you can't decide which niche to choose, take some time to create an Avatar of your ideal client. An Avatar is your pretend best customer; it will tell you his or her likes and dislikes, what they want out of life and how they work and operate. This could take a while so don't worry if you find this a very difficult exercise, but by completing it, you can then discover more about what you want to achieve in your business.

How to create your Avatar

Think about your ideal client and answer the following questions:
- Is your client male or female?
- Does it matter what sex they are?
- How old are they?
- How long have they been in business?
- What kind of business do they do?
- Do they work in an office or manual work?
- How do they communicate with you?
- How do they speak?
- What is their appearance?
- What kind of personality do they have?

If you find it difficult, try this exercise first:

Take a copy of a tabloid, for example, The Sun newspaper and write down the type of person that you think would read that paper. What kind of job do they do? What are their political views? How old are they?

Now take a copy of a broadsheet, for example, the Times Newspaper and repeat the same exercise.

Once you have your notes, this is an Avatar of the typical reader of that type of newspaper.' Now do the same for your business.

The Avatar for myPA is a man who is in his late 30s to early 40s. They have started their own business about two to three years ago, are in the process of expanding and know that they need some additional administrative support. Currently, the administrative support is being done by their partner who is getting fed up with spending all their time working on the business. He or she has very limited time to spend on social activities, and family life is suffering. My 'Business Avatar' has a very positive outlook on life and believes that anyone can become wealthy, that it is just about the amount of work and skills you have.

How to Use a Business Avatar

You could even use your Avatar when you need to make a decision about your business. Think about your Business Avatar; how would they react to your decision? Will it change your business? Will it change your services? Take your Business Avatar into consideration.

Whenever you create an entry on your blog, imagine your Avatar reading the entry. When you create a product, think how your Avatar would react. Could it be of use to him or her? Could they use the product?

Selecting Your Niche

As we covered in Section One, there are many different niches to choose from when you become a VA. Which niche you choose will depend on what skills you currently have, and what interests you. If you are good at accounting but don't particularly like it, you don't have to choose accounting and bookkeeping as your VA niche.

If you have always wanted to learn more about social media such as Twitter, Facebook and LinkedIn, take a course and find out more. There are plenty of learning opportunities on the internet. Do some work for yourself in these areas, and as you get proficient, you can then decide to specialise.

A niche doesn't just have to be about what kinds of services you offer. It can also be who you want to offer your services to or what specialities you want to offer. You may have experience of working within a specific industry which will put you a step ahead when trying to get work for that type of client. For instance, you may decide to offer a VA service to clients within the media community. Alternatively, you may want your niche to be internet marketing if you have a wide variety of internet marketing skills.

Be creative. Look at what industries may be able to use VAs, but may not even be aware of them. If you love art, you can bill yourself as an artist's VA and market your business to the artist community, and art gallery owners who know artists that could use help.

The beauty of being a VA and having your own business is that you can be whatever you want to be. You never have to take a job that isn't a good fit for you. Take some time and discover which niche is right for you.

What is Your Unique Selling Proposition/Point (USP)?

According to Wikipedia, a USP is:

"a marketing concept that was first proposed as a theory to explain a pattern among successful advertising campaigns of the early 1940s. It states that such campaigns made unique propositions to the customer and that this convinced them to switch brands. The term was invented by Rosser Reeves of Ted Bates & Company. Today the term is used in other fields or just casually to refer to any aspect of an object that differentiates it from similar objects." www.wikipedia.org.

A perfect example of a USP is the M&M brand of chocolate sweets. While there are many other similar manufacturers and products, M&M came up with the USP that "M&Ms melt in your mouth, not in your hand." While other sweets also had this same feature, M&Ms actually said it first.

Each and every advertisement must make a proposition to the consumer. It must not just be words or show-window advertising. It must say to the reader, "Buy this product, and you will get this specific benefit." When you think of M&Ms, you think, "Well, I won't be making a mess."

What will make your VA business more unique, more valuable, and more visible in the market? To be successful, you have to be unique and fill a special niche. One of the most common and harmful mistakes that small businesses make is not being unique, and therefore not positioning themselves as the best choice in the market.

By using a USP, you can demonstrate that your product or service is the best. Having a USP will substantially improve the positioning and marketability of your company and products.

Unique Your USP will clearly set you apart from your competition and will make you the most logical choice.

Selling Your USP will persuade a consumer to exchange money for your service.

Proposition Your USP is a proposal or offer suggested for acceptance.

Your USP can be the 'branding tool' that allows you to build a lasting reputation for your VA business. The ultimate goal of your USP and marketing is to have people say to you, "Oh, I've heard of you. You are the company who..."

This is a sign of a USP that works. Most importantly, a strong USP is what you will 'hang your hat on' for all your marketing and advertising efforts.

Here are some examples of winning Unique Selling Propositions. The examples show in industry what a typical 'blocker' (a problem that needs to be overcome) may be for a customer. The USP is how a company aims to overcome the potential customer's blocker.

Example 1 -- Shipping / Mailing Issues

Blocker: I have to get this package delivered quickly.

USP: "When it absolutely, positively has to be there overnight." (Federal Express)

Example 2 – Dental Industry

Blocker: Many people do not like to go to the dentist because of the long wait and the fear of pain.

USP: "We guarantee that you will have a comfortable experience and never have to wait more than 15 minutes, or you will receive a free exam."

So, what will it take to perfect your Unique Selling Proposition?

Client Retention

Client retention will be vital to the sustainability of your business. If they don't stay with you, you won't be in business for the long term. Client retention is vital to grow your business in another very important way: referrals. If you are keeping happy customers longer, they are more likely to tell their associates about what a valuable service you have offered them and how it has helped their business.

Client retention is covered in more detail in Section Four of this book.

Equipment Needs

While setting up a VA business may not cost much money, there are some basic equipment needs that you will have. Some will depend on the types of services you offer.

Computer The most important piece of equipment you will need is a computer, along with good broadband access. The majority of your work is likely to be done via the internet, and you don't want to be susceptible to 'down' internet service – this means not being able to connect with your clients, possibly missing vital communications, and also missing out on access to the hugely valuable resources of the internet.

Software and Programmes

Google Docs Google docs are extremely useful if you're providing diary management for a client. You can use Google Docs to share a calendar with your client so that you can see what their plans are. Google Docs also allows you to share documents for full collaboration.

Microsoft Office/Open Source You need to ensure that you have all the commonly used programmes such as Microsoft Word, Excel and PowerPoint.

Project Management System There are many project management systems available. Again, you will want to use something that is pretty accessible so that you can collaborate with clients if necessary. 'Basecamp' is an easy to use system with collaboration capabilities built into the software. 'JIRA' is a more powerful and robust system which is also available. You could also look at Asana, Wrike or Workzone. Microsoft Teams is becoming very popular. As a VA it is your role to keep abreast of the new project management systems on offer.

Printer A printer will be vital for your business and your clients' (depending on your services). There are many printers that also offer fax and copier facilities. These are an extremely space-efficient way to use a printer if you don't have the need for a large copier right away (which can also be very expensive in both initial and maintenance costs). As mentioned previously, see what your clients' needs are likely to be when you make the colour v. black & white decision). Remember, printing is a cost to you. If you are printing documents for your client ensure that you pass the charge on.

Telephone You will need a telephone to make and receive incoming and outgoing calls. Ideally, you should have a landline and a mobile. Times are changing, and with the cost of calls to mobiles being free and contracts now having unlimited calls, mobiles are becoming common as the only means of telephone communication. The decision to have a landline is very moot. I currently have a landline and mobile. Some of my clients would never call me on the mobile, others will only a mobile

Using the telephone is a cost to you; if you are making several calls on your client's behalf ensure you pass the charge on. Alternatively use a free service like Skype (there are some fees applicable, so be careful). There are many sites available that will give you a free landline number. However, the calls could cost a few pence more for the caller and yourself.

Audio Transcription Equipment If you are going to offer audio typing as one of your services you need to receive the audio file via e-mail. This means that you will need to be able to get the information digitally from your client. There are two ways you can get this audio typing off your computer and onto a piece of paper to be presented to your clients:

- You can type the words yourself, transcribing as you listen.
- Computer Programmes such as Dragon Naturally Speaking are available, which will automatically transcribe for you. Do be cautious if you are using one of these programmes. You will need to be trained, and you'll need to review the output before you send it back to your clients to ensure there are no mistakes.

This is a lot to take in, but it is not as difficult as it may sound and I hope that what we have covered in this section will see you well on your way to your own successful VA business.

Section Three

Marketing Your Business

As wonderful as it would be to have your phone ringing off the hook with new business, or have your email inbox flooded with new requests every day, the truth of the matter is you will need to market your business.

Even when business is booming, you need to be thinking ahead. All it takes is one client running out of money, and your income could suffer as well. You always want to have a full 'pipeline' of business through potential and regular clients. They are the ones you can talk to first when your business is in need of a shot in the arm.

Marketing comes in many forms, and we will be talking about several of them in this section.

Developing a Marketing Strategy

Marketing can be an awful lot of fun, or it can be incredibly frustrating. The most crucial part of marketing is having a strategy or plan. Just as you wouldn't get into your car and drive without having an idea of where you want to go and why you want to go there, you cannot market your business without a strategy. Think of it as your roadmap for marketing success.

As we have covered in the previous section, goals are crucial to your business's success, and this holds true for your marketing strategy. A good strategy will be broken down to long-term goals, mid-term goals, short-term goals and immediate goals.

For instance, your long-term goal may be to talk at a networking luncheon. That may be broken into an immediate goal of exploring different networking groups, a short-term goal of joining a networking group and a mid-term goal of asking for a place on the speaking agenda of an upcoming meeting.

The first step in developing a marketing strategy is to brainstorm all the possible marketing ideas you have. I have listed several in the following section, but you can also take a look online or at your local bookstore for additional ideas. Talk to successful business people and find out what worked for them in growing their business in its early stages. It is equally important to find out what didn't work. Learn from the mistakes of others and try to avoid making them yourself.

After you have made a 'laundry list' of all the marketing ideas you would like to try, you need to rank them. On a scale of one to five, which are the most important one to start? One should be the most important, and five the least.

Next, you should create a marketing calendar where you can list all your plans in date order. Start with the date that you want to have the marketing idea in place, and then move backwards to the milestones you will need to accomplish each marketing task. This will give you a good idea of what you can and cannot accomplish in a month. It's very tempting to want to put everything in place immediately. This just isn't possible. A good visual marketing calendar will show you what is feasible within a specific amount of time.

Ideas for Advertising Your Business

Listed below are some ideas for you to consider as part of your marketing strategy. There are various ways in which you can advertise your business.

1   Local Newspapers and Magazines. Many newspapers have a classified section that has an associated minimal cost. Some will even have a small 'services' section that costs slightly more but still, tend to be reasonable. The cost will go up as you look at display ads. The display ads can run anywhere from business card size to full page, and of course, the price will go up the larger you go.
2   Yellow Pages, Thompson Local and local directories (can be expensive to book a box advert, but one-line adverts are

generally free). It is sad to say that these forms of advertising books are becoming scares due to the internet. Yellow pages is now online under 192.com. Checkatreade is becoming very popular for trades.

3   Advertise on the internet, including the free listing sites, for example:

- www.freeindex.co.uk
- www.yelldirect.com
- www.thomsondirectories.com
- www.kyotee.co.uk
- www.hotfroguk.co.uk

4   For most free listings, you will include your business name, address (unless you are working from home, in which case you may want to consider leaving out the street address and just put the city), phone number, fax number, email address and website address. Some listings will let you put a brief explanation of your business. Think of how you can best describe your services in one or two sentences.

5   Local advertisements, for example, newsagents' shop window.

6   Appearing on the radio. Again, look for a compelling angle to get interviewed. It takes a little work, but email, call and mail local radio stations, letting them know you have a story their listeners may want to hear. Target radio stations that commuters listen to and have a good following. Listen to call in shows. If there is something that is relevant, call in and give your opinion and of course, the name of your business.

7   Putting leaflets through doors (businesses and people)

8   Promote a local event

9   There are always events looking for sponsors. Sometimes the donations can be a reasonable amount of money – you may even be able to donate something like water bottles or a food tray. In return, you can put your name in the programme, and perhaps even a small advert. Put together your own event that is relevant to your business. It could be an event on 'Smart Ways to Outsource'. You can rent a room at a hotel or check out the cost at your local library or other free venues. Invite

local businesses and put on a small seminar that delivers quality content. Of course, you can also let them know about your services. It's a great way for you to grow yourself personally and professionally, as well as growing your business.

10 Write a press release. Remember, when you write your press release you must be telling the newspaper or magazine that you have a wonderful new service that has not been thought of before; you need to make sure your article is not seen as purely an advertisement. This is a great way of getting some press in the local newspaper. Some newspapers and magazines need stories as fillers. Offer a compelling story to the Editor. It could be something like 'Going from Employed to Entrepreneur' or 'New Ways Businesses are Cutting Costs' and showcase how businesses can outsource their administrative work instead of hiring a new employee

11 Use your own car to advertise; stick on a magnetic logo or your telephone number. Various online print companies can create these; you just need to provide the design. Alternatively, create a poster with your business name and telephone number on it. You will need to make sure your car is clean and tidy at all times as it will be seen as an advertising board for your business and as I mentioned before, image is important.

12 Add comments at the end of web postings

13 Write free articles on a topic; become the expert - for example ezinearticles.

14 Run your own seminars/conferences. My first seminar was on time management, mentioned earlier in the book and a very important topic in my business and for my clients.

15 Start an email marketing campaign.

16 Become an approved supplier on your business colleagues' websites

17 At the bottom of any email add a small marketing message.

18 Brainstorm with your family and friends, who may have new ideas as to how you can market your business. You may be very surprised with the results.

19 Leave leaflets in prominent positions, for example at the local supermarket or library (always as permission before leaving your leaflets).
20 Attend workshops in business development.
21 Attend and join in job fairs and business promotional events.
22 Networking (this is covered in more detail later in this section).
23 Create personal profiles for yourself and your businesses on social networking sites, including:
    - www.ecadamy.com
    - www.linkedin.com
    - www.facebook.com
    - www.networkingforprofessionals.com
    - www.twitter.com
    - Start your own blog

Website

In this age of internet-savvy people, it is vital to have a website. When I first started, I was adamant that I didn't want a website, but I changed my mind very quickly. People wanted to know who I was and what I offered and demanded to have a look at my website. I had to create one very quickly. When you create your first website, don't be frightened about technology. You can get a website up-and-running very cheaply and very easily. Don't get conned into spending hundreds or even thousands of pounds on a very functional website that actually is above what you need at the time. I mentioned WordPress earlier which is a tool you could use yourself, for minimal costs, if you are confident enough to do so.

One common mistake that people make with their website is the philosophy of 'if I build it, they will come'. In other words, they simply use a website as a gigantic business card. It is important that your website is search engine optimised so that people can find you…even if they don't know they are looking for your business name.

As I mentioned before, you will want a website name (URL) that clearly defines who you are. If possible, use your business name. If that is not possible (if it is already in use), try to find a

50

shortened version or a variation of the name. Some other key points of an optimised website include:

- Keywords These should be included throughout your website. Think about what people would be searching for on the internet if they need the services you provide. For instance, the words 'personal assistant', 'virtual assistant', 'customer service', 'administrative services', for example.
- Pay particular attention to meta tags and meta descriptions.
- Have a strong 'opt-in'; a reason that people will want to sign up for a mailing list or newsletter or free report. This gives you the opportunity to capture someone's name and email address (with their permission) to use at a later date for marketing. An example of this which is often used is entering people into a free prize draw.
- Have your phone number clearly visible, and if possible a freephone number.
- Have a 'contact us' button or page where it is easy for potential clients to submit a question.
- List your services and a page about you.
- Include testimonials from clients that have used your services or past employers. Anyone that can say how great you are.
- Include details of any awards, community service or community groups that you belong to and what you get of of the groups.
- Have a short video where you introduce yourself and explain your services.
- (This is a great way to gain internet exposure).
- Have a blog on your website that lets you give daily tips or thoughts.
- Don't use gaudy flash or animation – this makes your page hard to load, irritates the possible client, and it is more likely they will move on to another more user-friendly site.

At the time I had convinced myself I did not want a website, it was largely because I thought it was going to be far too expensive. Here are a few key points that I experienced:

1   I made the decision that I could tell everyone that was interested in my services what I could do. I learnt very quickly that almost everyone will go to your website to 'check you out' before they decide to talk to you about the services you have to offer.

2   Once I discovered that I needed a website, I handed the decision over to some web developers, who to their credit created a wonderful website for me. I was very pleased with the look and feel. I did find the words difficult to write, but eventually, I managed to put some together that suited my personality and the company's structure. What I didn't realise was that if I wanted to change some of the words on the website I would have to ask the developers to change them and it would cost me a small fee each time. This was an added expense that I hadn't thought of or even considered. There are many developers who will design a website for you that will give you instant access to change the narrative on the site. When you decide to create a website, it is imperative that you have this function. You will also need to have the ability to create additional email addresses.

3   I have mentioned this already but cannot reiterate enough how essential it is to take the time to think about a proper domain name which should contain the name of your business where possible. Do not leave this to your web developer. This is your business; you need to be in charge of finding a domain that is relevant. You want a name that is easy for people to remember, and easy to spell and type. For instance, bestteammom.com has a double "t" and double "m" that is easily mistyped. You can find available domain names at www.1and1.co.uk or Godaddy.com. It is advisable to pick up the variations if you can afford it. For example, if your domain is a '.uk.' ending, you should look into buying up the '.net.', '.com,', or .org endings with the same name so that you don't end up with a competitor who has a near-identical web address. It is possible to 'point' these other web addresses to your main site so if somebody is looking for you

and types wrong ending; they will still end up at your main site.

Newsletters

Whether online or offline, newsletters are a fabulous way to advertise your business to both potential and current customers. Always make a newsletter something that is informative and a little fun. Something that a customer will look forward to reading the next time they see it has arrived in the mailbox or inbox, not something that they will recycle/throw away/delete without a second glance. Make it short and to the point but have a few key parts that are consistent in each newsletter. Some consistent sections could include:

- A key tip for time management (everyone can use this).
- A business news story (short and relevant).
- A client 'highlight' – choose one of your current clients and include a little about them – after seeking their permission to do so. This is a boost for them (and free advertising), and it lets your potential clients know how much you care about your existing ones.
- A motivational quote.
- A funny administrative/business story.
- Testimonials from clients (again with their permission but offer to include their business name and website - they'll be happy).
- An offer for new clients.

Please remember you must comply with GDPR rules. If you have not been given permission to send an email to the recipient, do not do so. Having an opt out at the bottom of a newsletter is not enough to use someone's email.

Business Cards

Creating a business card can be a very personal piece of marketing for your business. Nothing is more frustrating than chatting with someone, mentioning your business, getting them interested in your services but when they ask for a business card, having to tell them, "Oh my goodness, I don't have one..."

The most important point of a business card is to let people know your name, know that you have a business, and how to contact you.

Digital Business cards are now becoming popular and if you get an opportunity to get one, I advise you do. Not only will it save on paper, but you can also include a video and more information about you and the services you offer.

Creating your Business Card

After spending many, many hours creating CRM (Customer Relationship Management) systems (basically entering the details from business cards onto databases for my clients), I have created the following list to help with designing and creating the perfect business card (in my opinion):

1   Make sure your company name is clear and easy to read.
2   Use a clear and simple font for the company name and any other text - no fancy fonts that can't be read.
3   Do not use a personal email address like al-and-kate@fsmail.net. Be professional; purchase your company's domain name, even if you only use it for emails.
4   Use a font size that can be read by someone with poor eyesight. You want your potential clients to contact you and use your services. Don't make it hard for them to contact you.
5   Do not make it difficult for the reader to distinguish the name of your company, and if you use a tagline, please make sure it is appropriate. I have come across a business card that read 'Browns - Love Business'. This business was not an 'Adult' business but Business Coaching. Remember first impressions count.
6   Put your address on the card; you should have nothing to hide.
7   Put your full postcode. This shows attention to detail which is very important in a VA.
8   Put your full county on the card, for example, use 'Oxfordshire' and not 'Oxon'. To my mind, if you use shortcuts in your marketing material, it suggests you may be happy to take shortcuts elsewhere in your work.

9   Put a landline number of the card if you have one. If you use just a mobile number, it can indicate that you are a 'one man band'. Even if you are, you don't need to let the world know. You can get some 0845 numbers that will divert to your mobile number. A little research on this will pay dividends.

10 Create a card that is easy to store, not one that has to fold over two or three times.

11 Ensure the look of the card is appropriate for your field of business and that it tells the reader what you do for a living. Having only your name and address may be informative to you, but think of the reader, three, four or six months down the line. Are they going to remember your business?

12 Make sure your web address and email address are the same, e.g. '.co.uk' or '.com', not a mix of both.

13 Do not abbreviate words, e.g. 'Rd.' for 'Road'.

14 Make sure the paper you use is of a good quality.

15 Make sure the card is easy to read, for example, it is not see through. It may seem 'fun' or 'funky', but it can be distracting to the client. You want to make it as easy as possible for your client. You also want them to remember you as being professional, not funky.

Most importantly, read your business card design before you send it to print, and then get someone else to read it. Make sure the address is spelt correctly, and the telephone number(s) are correct. Double check your website address and then your email address. If you get the chance, put it aside for 24 hours and then come back to it and check it again. It can be easy to miss mistakes when you have been working on something yourself.

The Art of Following Up

One key aspect that many businesses brush aside too easily as not important is the art of following up. Keep a good record of every advertising avenue you use, what the results are, and what potential clients you have. Remember, someone may have REALLY enjoyed talking to you about your services and realised they need them, but the timing was wrong. A few months down the line, the timing could be just right. However, they may no longer have your name, phone number, website, email address for example, handy, and so will not be able to get in touch with you.

I often tell people when they think of marketing to 'put your consumer hat on'. Think of how many times you have received something in the mail or in your email and thought you would be able to use it or would like to look into it further, at a later date. As time goes on, other priorities come along, and the email, paper or letter is forgotten. Alternatively, it is lost in your ever-increasing inbox or pile of post, and you don't have the time to dig it out.

Where this is the case if someone were to follow up with you, wouldn't you be grateful? Give your potential clients this same opportunity. Never think of following up as 'bugging' someone; instead, think of the service and opportunity you are creating for someone.

Make sure you have a good Customer Relationship Management (CRM) system in place. For many people, this is a software programme. There are plenty available out there. Even something as simple as Microsoft Outlook can be used if you don't have money in the beginning. If you are a tactical person, a good filing system (which could be as simple as a small 4 x 6 recipe-type box) may be perfect for you. Make sure you include the person's name, their business, what they do, what services you may be able to help them with, a phone number and email, and notes of when you contacted them (by phone, email or mail). Also details of any noteworthy conversation – regarding business or any personal details which may seem worth remembering for future contact.

Any time that you are in contact with someone make a follow update. If you talk with them in person, ask permission to check in with them in a few weeks to see if they need anything. Few people will say no. If you are sending an email or piece of mail, note the date, and then set a follow-up date to call or email them.

It is vital that you action any follow updates that you make. Failure to do so will show that you may not follow up with deadlines and will put clients off working with you.

Social Media

In today's marketing world, social media is key to the success of your business. Social media is connecting with people via the internet in a type of social 'club'. New social media networks pop up each and every day. Some have staying power, and some do not. Most are free and worth a try; you never know who will find you and want more information about your services. Here are a few social media marketing avenues that are well worth your time and effort to market your business:

LinkedIn.com This is a professional network where you can build a profile (including current work position, previous career; as much or as little as you wish to include) and connect with other business people. Once you build your LinkedIn profile, search for others that you have worked with or for in the past, and invite them to join your network. This is all about making connections. You can (and should) load your CV to your profile, which will help you to connect with even more people.

As soon as possible, ask for recommendations from those you have worked with and use those recommendations on your linkedin profile. (You can also use the recommendations when sending out quotes, on the footer of your emails). This increases your profile on LinkedIn and also helps people to find you on the internet. You can even get video recommendations created. This is highly successful for many people.

Twitter Often thought of as a tool for the 'younger generation', Twitter is very popular throughout the world of celebrity as well as general business and social circles. Many people who are looking for virtual assistants are 'tweeters' – they are entrepreneurs who are familiar with using Twitter for their business purposes. Sending 'tweets' through your Twitter account not only shows that you are a good marketer but also showcases a valuable skill to potential clients.

Facebook This is another valuable social network to use for growing your business. Although you can use your personal Facebook account, I don't suggest this is a good idea. Mixing business with personal Facebook can sometimes be awkward, and downright embarrassing. That old friend from high school could post something just joking around that looks very unprofessional.

I would recommend creating a separate Facebook page for your business. Encourage specific friends and colleagues to become 'fans' of your page. You can then send out postings to the fans of your page letting them know of business-related tips, events and special offers.

Blogs Become a noted expert by posting comments on blogs throughout the internet. Do a search on blogs for business-related topics. When you find a relevant question, post an answer. Always be sure to include your business name and email address.

Networking

I want to discuss networking, which I believe, in its widest definition, within a business function is:

'meeting people that you wouldn't normally meet, in a business setting, at a predefined time and location, who happen to own a business.'

Objectives of Networking

Networking is about building relationships with potential clients, existing clients, your suppliers and your co-workers. At the end of the day, people prefer to do business with, and refer business to, people they know and trust.

One of the golden rules of networking is that you are not networking to the person that you are talking to; you are networking to his or her clients. I know that this is a very strange premise to appreciate but once you understand this fundamental concept you could become a first-class networker. Networking is all about small talk. The philosophy behind networking is all about creating relationships.

Networking can also be an excellent source of information for you and your business. You could find new ideas relating to your business, events, trends, opportunities and industry news. You can also find support or get collaboration for a proposed businesses idea.

Purpose of Networking

When you network, remember that you have decided that you are going to invest some of your very valuable time and effort out of the office meeting people who could potentially help your business grow. You are spending time away from making money and investing that time in promoting your business. Treat a networking meeting just like any business meeting you would attend; have a private agenda to this meeting.

For example:
- Set yourself an objective for each networking event. Be specific, e.g. I want to speak to ten new people.
- Decide what you are going to promote within your business.
- Determine what you would like to get out of the meeting on a personal level, e.g. building your confidence in meeting people.

Types of Networking Group

There are two types of networking meetings: formal and informal.

Formal meetings are those that are organised and have a purpose. Informal networking meetings are those that happen in the pub or during an idle chat with someone. Some examples of formal networking meetings include:

- BRX (www.brxnet.co.uk)
- BNI (www.bni-europe.com)
- Ecademy (www.ecademy.co.uk)
- Local Breakfast Clubs (Search local websites for these addresses)
- Local Dinner and Lunch Clubs (Search local websites for these addresses)
- Online Networking Groups (Various; check the internet)
- 4Networking (www.4networking.biz)
- Bizlinx (www.bizlinxinternational.com)

Once again, this list is not exhaustive. I would recommend that you look online for a list of networking groups in your area. If you find some difficulty in locating a networking group, you could always contact Business Link who will be able to advise you.

The Cost of Networking

Most formal networking groups will have a cost associated with them. In 4 Networking and BNI there is an initial joining fee, which can range from £200 to £500. You will then be expected to pay your annual subscription which can range from £250 up to £1000 per year. In addition to this, there will also be a weekly, fortnightly or monthly fee to cover room hire, food and beverages. For many of the more expensive networking clubs, you are permitted to attend two or three meetings without joining.

Many of the weekly meetings (for example BNI) will expect you to attend every week without fail. If you are unable to attend a meeting you are required to send a substitute in your place (you will be expected to pay for your substitute's food and beverages). Some of the networking groups will also expect you to donate some of your working week to finding business referrals or jobs for fellow members of the group.

Some of the local networking groups may not charge a joining and annual fee, but you will still be expected to pay a weekly, fortnightly or monthly fee, depending on the frequency of the meetings.

I know that this sounds very expensive, especially when you are starting up your business, but the confidence and training you gain by attending networking meetings cannot be underestimated. It is an ideal ground for you to discuss your business, to find out what is going on in your local business area and to find lucrative contracts that you may not have come across if you had not been talking to other businesses men and women.

What to Expect at a Formal Networking Meeting?

Going anywhere where you don't know anyone is very scary. This is no different for a formal networking meeting. Formal networking often has an order to the proceedings; a structure that is adhered to at every meeting, leadership, and relies on its membership to organise the club. There could be eligibility criteria for membership and the need for self-funding.

When you arrive at a networking group, in most instances you will sign in and pay your entry fee. This can be anything from £5 up to £35, depending on what time of the day you are meeting and where. Do not forget to pick up a receipt for this. You will then go into the meeting room, and it is up to you to start to talk to various people within the room.

Generally, you will be given 30 minutes to introduce yourself to the people in the room and find out about them and vice versa. You will then be asked to take a seat where the formal part of the meeting will then take place. Depending on the type of meeting you will be called up to conduct your 60-second presentation. This could be as short as 40 seconds and is also known as your 'elevator pitch'. There are a number of other names for this presentation, but ultimately you are given the opportunity to stand up and tell the people in the room about you and about your business.

The general rule of thumb is to state your name, state the name of your business, the type of business you are running and then a little bit about your business identity. Listed below is an example of a 60-second presentation. Please don't worry about your 60 seconds. This is an opportunity for you to tell the world how proud you are that you have decided to go into business, that you are open for business and all they need to do is come and talk to you.

Your 60/40 Second Presentation or Elevator pitch

The 60/40 second presentation is a brief description of you and your business and is generally equal to about 100 to 150 words.

A good 60/40 second presentation should include the following details:

- Who are you and what is your company called?
- What product or service you are offering?
- How the product or service will benefit your listener
- What your listener should do to get the product or service
- Finish by reiterating your name and your company's.

Below are two examples of a presentation that are specific to myPA, offering Virtual PA and Recruitment Services.

Example One

'Good Morning, my name is Julie Farmer, and I run a company called myPA. We offer 'Pay as you go' secretarial services. Our services include Credit Control and Audio Typing to Diary Management. This week one of my clients was on his way to a meeting and got lost. He called us, asked us to email him directions that he could pick up on his Blackberry and also to contact his client and let them know he was running late. Our client was happy because we provided a valuable service to him and his client was happy as he was kept informed of the situation. So if you know of anyone who needs a virtual PA or secretary, please give them my number: 01367 246003. My name is Julie Farmer from myPA, 'Pay as you go' secretarial services.'

Break down of the 60 Seconds

Who are you	Good Morning, my name is Julie Farmer
What is your company called	and I run a company called myPA,
What is the product or service you are offering	We offer 'Pay as you go' secretarial services. Our services include Credit Control and Audio Typing to Diary Management.
How will the product or service benefit your listener	This week one of my clients was on his way to a meeting and got lost. He called us, asked us to email him directions that he could pick up on his Blackberry and also to contact his client and let them know he was running late. Our client was happy because we provided a valuable service to him and his client was happy as he was kept informed of the situation.

Restate who you are	Once again, my name is Julie Farmer
What should your listener do to get the product or service	So, if you know of anyone who needs a virtual PA or secretary, please give them my number: 01367 246003.
Who are you	My name is Julie Farmer
What is your company called	from myPA, 'Pay as you go secretarial services.

Example Two

'Hello, my name is Julie Farmer, and I work for myPA – your local virtual personal assistants and recruitment consultants. We specialise in providing total employment solutions to young and growing businesses. We are able to take some of your administrative worries away from you whilst you continue to provide the product or service that you specialise in. We cover that niche in the employment sector where you know that you need additional support but don't want to take on a permanent employee. We can also provide temporary or permanent members of staff. If you find that you are spending too much time in your office and not out doing what you do best, then give me a call. Once again, my name is Julie Farmer from myPA.'

There is no need to say any more than that, and you can then sit down. It is also important to be proactively listening when others are giving their elevator pitch. Take notes on who may need your services based on their elevator pitch. Write down their names and telephone numbers or write down their names and go and talk to them afterwards. Get their business cards if at all possible. Let them know you would like to meet them at a later date convenient to them when you can discuss their business and what services you can offer to help them.

As with anything, you need to test and measure what you say about your company and what promotional material works for you. Example number two says all the right things, but doesn't really give a clear picture of how the service could benefit the listener; in effect, it doesn't take a problem that the listener could have and offer a solution to that problem.

Ultimately, your 60-second presentation will be one that suits your style, suits your services and is something that you feel happy and comfortable saying in a room full of people.

Play around with your presentation, it is common for people to read from a crib sheet. If you can avoid it, I would recommend this. If not, do not worry. Ensure your presentation is the best you can make it.

What to Expect at an Informal Networking Meeting?

Informal networking is probably the most effortless kind of networking that you will undertake, but never underestimate the power of informal networks. Informal networking can provide you with a major advantage when looking for new clients or contacts.

Informal networking is based on the principle of a shared exchange of information. There are limited rules to the meeting and advice is freely given and exchanged. This is in effect 'The Old Boys Network/Club'.

Informal networks groups can be difficult to define. The network group could be a group of colleagues or friends with a common interest. Other networking groups may be created through people you meet while travelling, attending church functions or simply someone you meet at the pub.

As a business owner, you are never off the clock. Any opportunity to promote, market or sell your business is an important marketing opportunity. Do be careful though; you don't want to bore your family and friends every time you meet them. Use your common sense when you are in an informal networking environment.

Networking Etiquette

Dress to impress
We have already covered just how important and long-lasting first impressions are, and this is certainly the case when it comes

to networking events, especially when you are starting up and growing your business. The impression of you and your business and how your business can perform is based on what people see. To make a good impression, ensure that you are well groomed and feel good about what you are wearing at all times. As you are advertising Virtual PA services, make sure that you turn up to a meeting appropriately dressed. In my personal opinion (and I am very conservative in this one) jeans and a t-shirt will not do. Equally, I don't believe that a very low cut top is appropriate for a woman or an open shirt showing half a man's chest. Remember you are a business owner and representing your profession and your business. If you feel smart and professional, then your appearance and mannerisms will appear professional, and your confidence will increase.

Remember, when you are networking,
"... you are promoting your personal brand. Like any product, your packaging defines and differentiates who you are as a professional business person. Make sure your visual message matches your verbal message."

Aviva Shiff, co-founder of Spark Training & Coaching Associates

Handing out Business Cards

There are some network etiquette issues that should be addressed. Firstly always carry sufficient business cards with you, but only give them out when someone has asked for one. Don't walk around distributing cards to all members of the networking group and not taking the time to speak to the person you are passing your card to or getting one of their cards in return. Keep your business cards close to hand, where they are convenient and easy to get to if someone asks for one. Try and carry some cards in your jacket pocket or your handbag. Don't make it difficult to get to your cards as you could make the person asking for the card ill at ease. If you have your cards in easy reach, it also demonstrates that you are prepared and ready for any questions about you or your business. If you have been asked for your business card by someone, always ask for their card in return. Once you have their card, look at it and read the name of the company as well as the name of the person you are talking to, acknowledge them. If you ask for a business card you will hold the power during the conversation; it is up to you to ask the questions and find out about his or her business. Don't be frightened about asking questions; people love to talk about themselves and their business.

Small Talk

When you are at a networking event, remember that everyone there has also made the decision to spend some of their valuable time out of the office to network. Therefore don't monopolise any one person's time. It is a good rule of thumb to spend a maximum of ten minutes with each person. This should give you enough time to find out about them and their company, and for you to tell them about you.

If you are stuck for ideas about what conversations you should instigate, consider the following questions:

What sort of business do you do?
This question is intended to help you get to know someone. It is an open-ended question that shows the person you are talking to that you are interested in them, that you want to find out more about them and what they do.

How long have you been in business?
This question is intended to show that you have been listening to the answer above and that you have understood what has been said.

What kind of clients are you after?
This kind of question demonstrates that you have listened to what has been said and you have an understanding of the type of business they run. It also shows that you are keen to help them find new clients, thus demonstrating that you are a team player and are happy to share your contacts and clients with other businesses to help them, which in turn will help your businesses.

What areas of the country do you cover?

This indicates that you are thinking about the possibility of working with this person and it could also demonstrate their geographical capabilities. It could also give you an opportunity to introduce them to someone else in the same type of business in a different area where they could collaborate and thus improve their businesses offering.

Is it a family run business?

This question is a friendlier question, to find out about the history of the business, and also the current circumstances of the person you are talking to, are they the decision maker?

What do you love about your work?

This question is designed to find out more about the person you are talking to, about their likes and dislikes, what they are passionate about, and could lead to a conversation about their plans for the business's future.

How did you choose this line of work?

This question is designed to find out about their passions and what drives them.

What did you do before?

If the person you are talking to has just started his or her businesses, this is a very important question as it can give you an understanding of the person's career history.

How do you think we can mutually work together?

You may feel uncomfortable asking this question, but don't rule it out. You may be talking to someone who you could recommend to your clients, or his or her clients could be recommended to you. This is the type of question that could lead to collaboration or some residual income for you. Business synergy is very important and should not be underestimated.

Discuss non-work topics

If appropriate, ask them about their personal lives. In some instances, people will be happier to talk you about their family first rather than their business as they have just met you. Alternatively, mention something that is happening in the news. Try and stay away from politics, religion and morals.

Building a relationship can be difficult and meeting someone and talking to them about their business within the first five minutes of meeting them could be seen as being discourteous.

Asking open-ended questions gives the other person the opportunity to share the way they feel about something, or further help them with a problem they may be having it helps you build more rapport with them, which will lead to a better relationship. It is important to make the other person feel at ease and that you truly want to talk to them and get to know them further.

At the end of the conversation, say something along the lines of, "It was good to meet you and find out about you and your company. Perhaps we could have coffee in the near future to see if there is any synergy between us our companies."

I know this is a very long-winded sentence, but it is just an example of winding up a conversation that is polite and interested without being pushy. You will find your own way and your own words.

General Tips for Networking

Sustenance You could try to eat something before the meeting so that your attention will be focused on meeting people. This will also enable you to keep your hands free to shake hands and easily offer and receive business cards.

Tactical Positioning

"Avoid standing at the bar. People may congregate there, but it's not an ideal spot to engage people in conversation. Instead, stand near the food or dessert table where people are lingering and eating. You'll find them more open to talking because people like to chat during meals and people are usually happy and receptive when they have ready access to food."

Aviva Shiff

Follow up after a networking opportunity

Your connection may start at a networking event, but the relationship is built over time. It is important to follow up the first meeting in an appropriate fashion to keep the momentum going and stay at the forefront of people's minds. You can achieve this by email or personal note, "It was a pleasure meeting you. I'll call you in the next week or so to set up some time to get together."

Make sure you follow up with everybody you received a business card from, an email or telephone call is sufficient.

You can also stay in touch by periodically sending important information, articles or notification of a relevant, upcoming event. This demonstrates your understanding of a person's needs and your willingness to be of service. You can also set up a Google news alert and send congratulatory notes when you learn of pertinent deals or promotions.

Here is an example of what to include in a follow-up note:

It was good to meet with you at the {Event Name} on {Event Date}, and to hear about you and {Their Company Name}.

As promised, please find enclosed a leaflet describing the services of {Your Company Name}, which I trust you will find useful. In essence, we offer a number of services:

Service One	{description of service}
Service Two	{no more than 15 words}
Service Three	{no more than three points}

I would welcome the opportunity to learn more about {Their Company Name} and explore how we might help each other in the future.

Networking in Summary

There is a lot to think about regarding networking so, in brief, these are the key points to keep in mind:

- The object of networking is to introduce yourself to the business community and find out about the other businesses that could help you or which you could help.

- Networking can be formal and informal.
- Formal networking is joining local or online networking groups to advertise your business and find out about other businesses in your area.
- Informal networking is talking about your business in a social atmosphere, for example in the pub.
- Carry enough business cards with you at all times.
- When you meet someone ask about them and their businesses.
- Remember and practise your 60-second introduction about your businesses.

Exhibitions

Participation in exhibitions can be a fabulous way to market your business and put your networking skills to use. An exhibition can be business-related, or you can think 'outside the box'. For instance, having a booth or table at a health fair may be a way for healthcare professionals to learn more about your services. Be sure to have plenty of fliers that promote your service, put on your best attire and biggest smile, and be ready to talk and network.

Often it is helpful to have a small prize draw organised, in order to get as many business cards as possible. Your draw could be for a one-hour consultation on VA services. Just let people know that all they have to do is submit a business card to be eligible. For those who don't win, send an email or letter letting them know you would be happy to keep them on your newsletter list.

Exhibition Material

I created what I thought was a very comprehensive display of advertising material that made myPA look like the best company in the world... or so I thought. Below is an example of one of the posters I created

Your Office, Home, Your Life
We have the ability to work in your office
We are able to work from your home at your convenience
Assistance in taking control of your life
www.mypabusiness.co.uk
email: mypainfo@tiscali.co.uk
Tel: 07813 XXX XXX

Try not to use clip art. There is no question in my mind that a picture tells a thousand words. In this image, I was trying to say that you, my new client, are the boss; you work so hard, and you need at least three of you to get your daily work done, but don't worry, your answer is here. myPA is here to help you; we will ensure that your office procedures and administration are taken care of professionally and quickly, and you can carry on with your business activities.

What it actually says is 'we are a very young business and just trying to find our feet and have put this together on a computer on the cheap'.

What I was trying to say was, 'Look, I have a website: www.mypabusiness.co.uk - you could go and have a look at it. If you need my services, don't worry you can also contact me by email, here is my email address mypainfo@tiscali.co.uk'. What I actually said was, 'I have a website, but at the moment I don't know enough about the website to create an email from the website, so I have created this free email address from Tiscali'. In addition to that, take another look at the email address.

What I wanted to say was, 'This is the information email address for the services offered by myPA. Hence the email address is myPA info@tiscali.co.uk'. However, what everyone saw was 'my pain @ tiscali.co.uk'. How amateur this appears, I cringe every time I look at it. This was a lesson I learnt very quickly, and with any of my new clients or whenever I am out at a networking meeting (formal and informal), I will always point similar details out.

I kick myself every time I think about this one. Check all the information on any literature you send out. Put it to one side for about 24 hours if you can and then check it again. If you can, get someone else to check it for you. I created all my hand-outs, my business cards, my comp slips for example, with the wrong telephone number on it. I was one digit out, but this was more than enough for my potential clients to make me seem incompetent.

Article Writing

Make sure any article you write is full of helpful content, and not seen as just a glorified advert. Give some good tips. At the end, you will have a place to put your information as the author, so here you can include your business name and website.

Online

Writing and submitting articles online is one of the best ways that you can point people to your website. What most people do is use search engines such as 'Google' to find what they are looking for and to check you out. If someone enters, 'virtual assistant in UK' and your website doesn't show up until the 3rd or 4th results page, the chances are that they will have decided on someone before they even see your website.

Article writing, and distribution helps the search engines to 'optimise' your website. This basically means that the articles are telling the search engines that you are an expert on your subject matter. The more relevant articles you have, the more of an expert search engine will consider you, and the higher you will rank when a search is done for your services.

Every time you write and are published online, you should include your website address, or a link created on the article directing people to your website. The more links you have, the better. You will often hear this referred to as 'backlinks'.

A great place to publish articles is at www.ezinearticles.com. You can also find online magazines, websites and blogs that may be interested in publishing your articles.

With any article writing, you want to ensure that you are writing relevant content that is helpful to a reader. You can write about 'how to find a good administrative outsourced partner' or 'effective time management' - or anything else that may help a business owner. You can mention your business in the article, but don't overdo it. The end of article will be where you can put a blurb about you and your business. You are positioning yourself as an expert that people will trust.

Offline

It used to be that people thought they had to go through a 'traditional' publisher in order to get an article published. There are easy ways of self-publishing nowadays, and you can write an article or a short brochure that is helpful to business owners.

It can take a little more work to get published offline, but it is worth the effort. Any time you are published online or offline, your credibility soars.

Freelance Services

When you are first getting going with your business, getting the first few clients and establishing some credibility can be the toughest first step to overcome. You may want to consider starting off as a freelancer through one of the online freelance companies.

You may have to start off at a lower rate, but it will mean you are able to build a client profile and some testimonials fairly quickly. Success begets success. Once potential clients see you have an established clientele, they are more likely to use you. Getting those first clients can be frustrating and freelance companies are a great way to overcome that obstacle.

Most companies will let you join without a fee. Some will let you upgrade to a higher service or the ability to bid on more jobs with a fee. The payments are secure if you stay with the payment in the online company. Do not be lured to go 'offline' and make separate arrangements. You can get stuck doing work without getting paid.

If you decide to go with a freelance company, spend the time to create a quality profile. Let potential clients know a little about you and your services. Let them know what sets you apart from anyone else. Things like a quick turn around and full communication are important to potential clients.

When you bid on a job, do not send in a 'canned' bid, i.e. a blanket style bid for each and every job. Take the time to look at each job request and personalise your bid. Find something that you can connect with the client and use that connection.

Some online freelance companies to take a look at include:

- www.upwork.com
- www.Freelancer.com
- www.Odesk.com
- www.Fiver.com

Take a good look at the cost of each and any service fees. Try a few out at the lower price before going for any upgrades.

You may be tired now of hearing about marketing, but hopefully, this chapter has shown you just how much there is to think about and how you can use all these marketing tools to your advantage to create a successful and well-reputed business which clients keep coming back to and recommending you.

Client Management

Building Relationships

Most people want to have a very amicable relationship with their clients. You want to be on the best possible terms at all times. This requires work, planning, and always putting your best foot forward. Relationships take consistent work. We know that from any relationship we've had in our lives. A business relationship is similar in many ways to a friendship or a marriage. It takes communication, cooperation and commitment, to be a success.

In order to get to the point of how to be the perfect VA, we need to discuss the building of a solid foundation, setting expectations for both you and your client, and proactive thinking; the ability to think ahead and prevent problems arising.

The type of relationship you have with an employer or client will dictate the ease with which you will be able to work with them. It is vital that you build a level of trust and understanding from the very beginning of each relationship. This is your foundation, the building blocks of your future with your client. There has to be a level of trust on both sides.

As the VA, you must trust that your client will give you work in a timely manner, with clear and precise instructions. On this point, it may be worth ensuring that you have your client's instructions in black and white, to refer back to in the case of any dispute. You could ask your client to put their requirements in writing, or you could summarise your understanding of the job in an email (what the job entails, timescales, payment, for example), for them to review. This may not sound very trusting, but if viewed positively it is a way for both you and your client to ensure that you both have the same understanding. You could even record your meetings on a dictation machine; this would provide an aide memoir for you and your client. It could also provide an excellent piece of marketing research for you. During your conversation, you will hear again and again what your client's needs are and can then address your marketing material accordingly.

In turn, your client must trust that you will be responsible and deliver what is expected within a reasonable timeframe, which you must agree between you. They also need to trust that you will maintain good communication with them and alert them of any issues if and when they arise.

Some clients don't understand that in this world of internet searches and information at our fingertips, research still takes time. Scheduling takes time, and organising takes time. This is why your client needs a VA. They may not know what it takes to complete the task(s) they have requested of you; they just know it needs to be done. This can make for a somewhat unrealistic view of how and when things can be accomplished. It is all down to communication and setting expectations.

Expectations

Many clients will have been through several assistants, secretaries, or helpers of some kind or another. They may be frustrated with the lack of accountability and dedication they have found. It is your first order of business to set the tone of the relationship by being upfront about your expectations and in turn understanding theirs. Develop a list of work principles that you can convey to a client before the first task is even started. Let them know you intend to have all tasks completed in a timely matter. Set up a priority level that you can assign to each task so there is no question of where it should be placed on the 'to do' list. Let them know that you take your job very seriously. You need to show them that you respect their business and as their VA you are there to help them succeed. This will prove to them your level of commitment and reinforce your ability to tackle tasks head-on.

Never forget that this is 'their' business. If it was your business and your name was on the letterhead, you could make all the decisions. Your job, as a VA, is to determine the needs of your client so that you can smoothly pave the road ahead, leading them along the road to a successfully run business. You are the person behind the scenes helping it all run without a hitch.

I was working with a client who was trying to explain to me his expectations. He kept telling me about why his last VA didn't work. As I listened, it became clear that he may have been talking about the past, but he was still telling me about his expectations. He had tried to teach his last VA how to work his billing cycle and the precise way he tracked his hours to be billed to clients. It was actually a very simple process but required more hands-on work. His previous VA insisted that she rework the billing so that she could utilise her own software program. She didn't want to bend at all and was only thinking of how to make the job fit with what she knew. Needless to say, she was let go after a short period of time because they couldn't find a common ground on which build their working relationship. It was neither her business nor her job, to try to rework his billing to fit her needs. Remember, his business, his name on the letterhead. That's not to say that you may not have great ideas that can't be implemented down the road but don't start off with a new client trying to change everything that they have put in place up to that point. If you try to force your ideas on a client, you will meet an immovable front that will make every step you take in the future very difficult to overcome.

It is important to determine, up front, what the job description is, what time frame is expected for tasks, and make sure to always ask for items to be prioritised. It is very common for the priority list to change on a daily basis. What was a priority yesterday or earlier in the week may no longer be one today? As a VA you need to be adaptable and flexible enough to understand that your client's priorities could change on an hourly/daily basis.

I had a client who was consistently throwing numerous jobs at me. He would let me know at the time the priority of those tasks, and I would get to work. Three hours later he would call me with more tasks. I would add them to the list and continue on with the existing priorities. On one occasion, my client called me wanting a task finished that he had only given me at the end of the previous working day. I explained that I was completing the items on the list which he had already prioritised for me and that I would have the other tasks done within the next few hours. He calmly pointed out that the priority list from the previous day was no longer relevant once he had added the new items. A lesson learned. This is another time to ask questions. If your client calls with new tasks, let him know what you are currently working on and ask him to reprioritise the list you have. This may be another time to clarify with a quick email summary. Clarification is the only way to see and understand what is expected.

Under-promise and Over-deliver

Your best tool with a new client is to under-promise and over-deliver. This is a great way to gain the trust of your clients and let them know that you take this job seriously. Let's take the example of a client asking for their dissertation of 200 pages to be typed, proofed and sent back as soon as possible. You know that if you worked on this non-stop, you could have it back within the day. However, you let your client know that you will return it within 24-30 hours. When you actually have it back to them completed within 12 hours, they can see that you are extremely competent and have advanced a few steps in the trust level. Always give yourself enough time, allowing for interruptions and problems that may arise. You don't want to be known for promising something in 12 hours and it actually taking 30. It will happen from time-to-time; situations come up, and things get in the way, but make it a very rare occasion where you need to apologise for not making a deadline.

If you are constantly missing deadlines or you are turning in incomplete or sloppy work, you will come across as unreliable and not really caring about your job. You need your clients to know that they can count on you at every turn. When you can over-deliver it lets your clients know that they can count on you to follow through with any tasks they choose to give to you.

Assertiveness Skills

The ability to be upfront with your clients is also key to your success. Never be afraid to ask questions. It is better to have a job or problem explained fully rather than to fall short or, worse, misinterpret the expectations of the job at hand. A misinterpretation might cause you to deliver a product that is the complete opposite of what was originally expected. A client will admire your assertiveness as long as you treat them with a certain level of respect. They need to understand that you are only looking out for their best interests and wanting to produce the best possible outcome for their business. Remember, it's all about them.

The communication gap between individuals can be very large at times. It is up to you to bridge that gap and make the communication flow freely with your client. Make sure you are communicating on the same level and that you are listening as carefully as you are speaking.

One of my clients designs his own business cards every year; he likes to have a new design each year as he adds a calendar to the back of each card. Every year he grumbles about the cost of printing the cards. He inevitably asks if I can print them out for him. Every year I tell him that I can, but the quality would not be up to his standards, and he would be very disappointed in the result. This year we printed the cards using an online printer. I uploaded a Portable Data Format (pdf) file of the image he had created to the website and used their program to fix the image onto the card design he had chosen. My client saw the design before it was ordered and authorised it, as he had to do so before entering his credit card details for payment. Despite this, when he received the cards, he complained that the printers had cut ¼ of a centimetre off his picture. I reminded him that he had authorised the image and that he had known at the time of placing the order that the image was going to be cut in that way. Although he was still unhappy with the cards, he had to acknowledge that this was true.

An essential assertiveness skill is managing your client's expectations with regards to your time and availability. This can be tricky. Of course, you want to be available to your clients. You want to help them and do your job proficiently, but at the same time still, have a life. You have to appear to be available all the time but still, maintain your own space. The time you spend working and the time that is your own are very different, and you need to be comfortable enough to develop a line between the two. This is very important. This is not an area you need to be mean or argumentative in; it is just an area where you need to be firm. Regardless of who you work for, they don't own you. It is absolutely imperative that you set up boundaries very early in the relationship. There will always be exceptions. Just don't make them the norm. Once you've compromised your time, clients will not hesitate to leech over into your personal time over and over again. The last thing you want is a client calling you at all hours and interrupting your private time. This is something they will not hesitate to do unless you define your working hours.

When I first set up my VA business, I told my clients that I would be available 24 hours a day 7 days a week. I wanted my clients to know that I was looking after them at all times. It soon became apparent that my clients took me at my word and did call me any time. It has taken a long time for my clients to realise that I no longer work Sundays and that I will not answer the telephone late in the evenings.

You need to state upfront that you work from eight in the morning until five in the afternoon (or whatever you determine your set office hours to be) and that while you will not take calls after hours you have an answering service that they are welcome to leave a message on if it can't wait until the next business day. As a VA it is highly likely that you will have clients in several different time zones. They will, of course, want to reach you at different hours of the day. Let them know that you will respond to them within 12 hours during the business week and then determine if you will respond within 24 hours or less, during your off-time. Always be aware of the time differences but still be adamant about your hours and your availability. By being upfront from the beginning of your working relationship, you will ensure that your client understands and respects your boundaries.

Helping Define Requirements

Surprisingly, many people don't know what they want. It is easier for them to tell you what they don't want, or express what they don't like than to put into words exactly what it is that they do want. You should use your own series of questions to narrow down the selections and help your client shape their vision so that they can better relay it to you. This way you will be able to arrive at a more precise, clear-cut definition of the job at hand.

When your client tells you that they want the new letterhead the same blue colour as the sky, there is room for misunderstanding. Your best bet is to help them define which shade of sky blue they mean. Is it the blue from the morning sky? The blue of the sky at sunrise, or maybe the blue sky of dusk? Your ability to ask questions will help them define what they want and ensure that you go off to work confident of your client's requirements.

It is also extremely important to take clear notes, and save emails and other communications so that you can back up your case if something goes wrong.

You will quickly come to the realisation that most clients want to cut costs. They want a higher bottom line/a more profitable business. However, very few are willing to sacrifice quality to get there. You can almost always find a cheaper way of doing something, but you will need to determine beforehand if your client is willing to settle for below-par results. This is a great time to be thinking ahead and be proactive. There are so many occasions where money can be saved by successfully planning ahead. This way, the problem of having to cut corners because of cost is solved.

Since you are a VA, you can never assume that you understand your client's requirements. The first word in VA is 'virtual'. The majority of the time you aren't physically in the same office as your client so you must be very specific and use visual aids whenever possible to come up with a picture that you both agree is the same colour of blue. Just because you think the most beautiful shade of blue is the top of the ocean waters, you can't expect your client to agree. They may never have even seen the ocean. It will always come back to asking questions and defining your client's preferred shade of blue, not yours.

Dealing with Difficult People Professionally

You have to face the inevitable. No matter how long it takes, you will eventually find yourself in direct business with a difficult person. It may even be an extremely difficult person. To know how to deal with difficult people, you must first take the steps to understand the person and the existing situation. Usually, it's not the person themselves who are difficult; it's the situation that they have been put into that can change them into someone that most of society would automatically reject for such callous and ridiculous behaviour.

Deadlines, criticism, and inflexible situations can quickly make a person not just difficult to work with but absolutely unacceptable as a boss. As they are a client, you may not want to lose them, so you will need to find the best way to work with them and try and find out what has made them so stressed. You will need to handle each client differently; some with kid gloves and others with a strong fist. Just remember always to use grace and respect, stand your ground, and ensure that you are providing the best service you can and that your client gets the task completed to their satisfaction. If you find that you cannot work with this person, that's fine. You may politely suggest that you are unavailable to work with them on future projects due to other commitments. If you are able to find a replacement, then that could be an excellent solution.

As a VA, you may be an entrepreneur and your own boss, but you still need your clients to be profitable. Without your clients, you don't have a job, so you need to treat them as valuable assets. They are the reason you are working.

I had one client who was an expert procrastinator. It was absolutely inevitable that he would wait until the very last possible second to hand over a task. In every other aspect, he was the perfect client. He paid well, he was extremely personable, and for just those reasons I felt it was worth some extra time and investment to keep him as a client. Once I was able to determine some of the recurring tasks, for example creating mail outs every six weeks for a new promotion, or undertaking customer surveys, I could get a jump start on them and even begin to prompt him for content I needed to get the tasks finished. By giving this client constant attention I achieved excellent results for both of us.

Always try to understand the situation, where your client may be coming from, and what the situation at hand is all about. You will be surprised what you can accomplish with a soft voice and a gentle hand. You will then be hailed the hero and ultimate negotiator because you have proved your services invaluable by sifting and sorting through what your client considered to be an insurmountable task.

So many times, people will delegate tasks that they don't understand or don't want to deal with, simply to get them out of the way. In general, if something makes a person uncomfortable, they are less likely to deal with it. These are the jobs that get shoved under the carpet and then end up becoming last minute hassles. Make yourself someone who is willing to tackle the difficult or 'uncomfortable' tasks. In your client's mind, this makes the problem go away, and you look like a saviour in their eyes. Make yourself someone who is easy to work with and the one who always brings solutions and answers. Never complain or whine. Be a go-getter who is not afraid to take on tasks or problems. Be a problem-solver who is willing to tackle whatever is necessary and never be a part of the problem itself. These are tried and true techniques that will make you a much better and highly sought-after VA.

Accountability and Addressing Mistakes

Find a Personality Match

When it gels, it is like heaven. When you find a client, who can meld with you and your abilities it's a joy to work with them. It's not necessarily a rare occasion, but as a VA and a business owner, it is certainly worth looking for. It is something you are always trying to achieve. To work in harmony is not just enjoyable but makes jobs seem effortless and more manageable all the way around. The question is, how do you find that perfect match? Well, it's not as hard as you think. A lot of the time you will develop a better personality match just by making a more cohesive environment for your client. This will generate a wonderful working relationship between the two of you. If you spend time sifting through clients looking for that 'perfect' match, you will pass up many clients who could be building your personal business. There are a lot of good clients out there and with a little bit of shaping they will become great clients.

One thing to always remember is that you are not looking for a best friend or even a mother or father figure. You are looking for a client. You can develop a rapport with them that will make your working relationship easier just through friendly chatter. However, a client really doesn't want or need to hear about what you did over the weekend or what your child accomplished at his last sporting event. You have to keep it professional. Never confuse the lines between friendship and client. There needs to be a distinct line drawn in your client relationships. On the other hand, your client may tell you about his weekend, what happened to his children or his concerns. Be interested and try to remember a couple of details where you can, e.g. a child's name or your client's interest in golf. Taking an interest can strengthen any relationship, whether business or personal.

Don't be quick to judge. When you get a new client, it's a courtship. There is always a 'getting to know you' period. It's sometimes a slow and steady process that takes time and patience. You must allow yourself that time to get to know your client's personality and let them get to know yours. You need to give it time so you can understand their quirks and work out the details.

Whenever I start with a new client, I go through a series of questions with them. It's more just to get them talking. I like to get a feel for their business. For example:

What do they do? It may sound simple, but I like to get an in-depth analysis of what my client's business entails. I have a client who I thought dealt with marketing, however, once I got through my first question I realised the company does so much more than just simple websites or newsletters. They were creating posters, mailing samples, printing DVDs and CDs, workbooks and business cards, for example. Most people like to talk about themselves and, likewise, clients often enjoy talking about their business, especially if it is an area of particular interest or passion for them. Understanding a client's business can often make your job as a VA easier, as the tasks you undertake make more sense.

What is the company history? Learn how long the business has been running and how it has grown over time. Is it just beginning? Has there been a partner change?

What is the company vision? You want to know where your client sees the company going in the next six months, three years and five years. This way you can know what their focus is and help them achieve their goals.

Is there a job description for your role? Keep in mind that this will always be changing and evolving. It is a good idea, even if it has already been stated, to get a better breakdown of what they think your job should entail.

A good tip once you have been working for a client for a month or so, is to ask for an evaluation of your work for them. Repeat this after you have worked for them for six months. This will highly impress your new client. It lets them know that you take their business and your business seriously and will also create an open arena for honest feedback which will enable you to realise which areas you are doing well in as well as those which may require more work. By giving your client this opportunity, you are enabling an even stronger relationship between you.

As you are going through your list of questions, take careful notes. You can then refer back to these time and time again. Once you've got some history on the company from your client, it's even a good idea to do some brief internet searching on your own. Your client will never tell you everything. I'm not telling you to do an entire background check on your clients. Just compile a little information. It is true to say that knowledge is power. Don't take everything you read to heart, however, because there is as much bad information out there as there is good.

I once had a client who wanted me to go through old files to compile a list of articles he could use in an upcoming book. I was given several topics to research, and that was about it. I spent several days scouring files to come up with wonderful articles. When I presented the list to my client, I found out that some of the articles I had pulled were written by a past partner and were unusable. If I had done prior research, I would have known that there had been a breakup and to avoid articles by his past partner.

A great idea and a professional habit is to arrange a 30 day trial period in which either party can dissolve the arrangement without obligation. This offers an easy way to walk away if needed. It can be like trying on a pair of shoes to see if they fit. You have to stand in them, sit in them and look in the mirror to see if they will feel good on but will be the perfect fit as well.

After 30 days, if it doesn't feel right, you should feel free to invoke your 30-day arrangement. There's no point trying to cram a square peg into a round hole. You don't have to do this in a way which will form ill will on either side. It's a mature and well-adjusted person who can accept that a relationship isn't working and move forward. Don't jump the gun however and think that just because you didn't meld on the first task, you need to scrap the entire client relationship. Try again, using different techniques. Remember through your assertiveness you can ask questions that will help better define your client's requirements. On a rare occasion, you will find someone you will not be able to work with, whether it is because their demands are unrealistic or that the lack of appreciation is beyond the threshold of tolerable, whatever the case, a job is not worth pain and suffering when it just doesn't work. You don't want is for a bad relationship to affect the good relationships you have with other clients.

If you ever get to a point where you do have to part ways with a client, you should do your absolute best never to burn bridges. If you have kept up your work ethic, your client will know that you won't bad-mouth them, or their company. It can be simply stated that the arrangement isn't working out and that you need to put your efforts into other clients. This is a small world we live in, and there may come a point where you have to cross that bridge, even if it is only to reach the other side. A burned bridge takes a long time to repair and is never very stable. Run your business in a way that will allow you to hold your head high, day in and day out. It has a lot to do with integrity and moral values.

Maintaining Positive Client Relationships

After finding that perfect client you now want to keep them as long as possible. I cannot stress enough; it is important to follow up and follow through. This is how you sustain a very profitable business. It is all about how you conduct yourself and manage your business. You HAVE to be reliable, and dependable.

It's never just that one client that you are maintaining. You have to understand the importance of this because anyone client will lead to more clients and more clients. I'm pretty sure you see where this lead. One happy client will provide you more future business than any advertisement you can purchase. Word of mouth is your best form of advertising.

A big step in maintaining positive client relationships is becoming a good listener. You need to pay attention to not only your client but everything around your client. By listening to what he talks about and how he talks about it, you will be able to obtain a lot about their character, and their likes and dislikes, not to mention how they prefer to have situations handled. Second to asking the right questions is listening to the answers. It is very important to keep your mouth closed and your ears open.

If there ever comes a time when your client doesn't need your services anymore, as long as you have been an exemplary VA, then they will go so far as to help you find your next job because you have proven to be a valuable asset.

Be Proactive/Be Indispensable

To be that perfect VA that everyone wants to keep around, you must form a bond with your client that makes them feel that if that bond were ever to sever, then their business would be mortally wounded. You have to become, the 'Jeeves to their Wooster'. Your position must be able to surpass a definition. The definition of 'assistant' is one who assists. It doesn't clarify what you will be assisting in. So be prepared to do it all and do it all very well. Even if you are asked to do a job or task that falls outside of your expertise, do not say 'I can't'. Become the assistant who will find someone who can. A client doesn't want to hear 'I can't' or 'I don't know how'. They just want to tell you what to do and then have it done! Become the person who can get it done for them. So, do the research on how to get the problem solved by someone who is capable. You are then taking care of the situation, which is what a good VA should do.

One of my clients asked me to help him put together an exhibition. He is an artist and needed some plinths to show some of his portfolio. Obviously, I couldn't make these plinths myself, so instead of going back to him and saying I couldn't do it, I recruited the help of some fellow entrepreneurs and made it happen. The result was amazing, and my client was thrilled with the finished exhibition. It really didn't matter to him who did it or how it got done, just that it did, and it was done successfully.

It is vitally important for you to be a proactive person. It takes so much time and energy to run around putting out fires that could have been avoided by taking care of them before they became a problem. It's all about looking ahead, instead of looking to the past. You have to be able to look ahead and remove any obstacles that may prevent things from running smoothly.

There are some situations where you shouldn't have to wait for instruction. You need to take initiative on your own. For example, you have a client who has a presentation to do next Friday. You know they will need presentation folders made up, you can take the initiative to find the folders, find the artwork, find the content, and have it all prepared to be proofed before the presentation day comes around. Once again this would be the perfect time to ask questions, to find out what is needed for that day. You have to remember to look ahead. It's never a fun place to be when you have to scramble to get work done continually. Plus, as mentioned earlier, a lot of the time when you look ahead and plan for upcoming events, you can save your client money. Every client likes that to happen.

Professionalism, Confidentiality and Integrity

If you have integrity, you never talk about one client with another. That would be an automatic red flag to a new client that you can't keep your mouth shut. Hearing you talk about your existing clients will just make any potential new client think that you will do the same with them. Aside from the fact that nobody likes to be talked about behind their back, there are professional issues of confidentiality, especially if your clients work in a similar field. You could give away product secrets or other valuable information which could affect their ability to win or lose business themselves.

Keep office secrets to yourself and always be discreet. It is not your place to talk. If a client is running their business in a way that makes you uncomfortable, then that's another topic and one which you need to deal with yourself. You must keep your clients' confidentiality at all times; it is just what a good assistant would do.

Section Four

Finances

When you are starting your Virtual Assistant business, you need to be realistic about the amount of money that you will be making. Please take note that it is unrealistic to think you will be able to take your previous corporate salary of, for example, £50,000, and divide it by 52 (the number of weeks in a year), times that by 40 (the number of hours in a working week) and come up with an hourly rate to charge your clients. It just doesn't work that way. You can't equate what you had in corporate life to what you will have as a VA. There are many other factors you will need to consider.

Cost of the product

You are the product. Your time will be what the client is paying for and wha you offer. Of course, there may be some ancillary costs that you bill for, such as postage, or cost of adverts that you may run on your client's behalf. These costs can depend on what your speciality or niche is as a VA.

What you can charge

You may vary your method of charging depending upon the type of work you are taking on. You could choose to charge per hour, which some clients prefer. You should set your rate, however, be cautious about publishing a firm rate on any printed material; the rate you set today could be far too low or far too high. Remember that any rate can become negotiable. You may be able to offer a discount if you are going to be working long term for a client. Equally, if it is a quick project where your client needs a fast turnaround, you may be able to charge a premium price.

Another option is to charge a set fee for completion of a project. Again, do not make the mistake of locking yourself into a set published price. If you are bundling several projects together with a client, you may be able to afford to give them a discounted price. If you are agreeing a project fee, then this is a good time to employ the rule of setting the boundaries (or 'scope') of the project in writing. This way there should be no 'scope creep' where the client changes their mind about what the project entails, causing far more work than was originally agreed. If the project starts to grow, then you can refer back to the original agreement and negotiate a new price.

Cost of your overheads

Your overheads include EVERYTHING that you must pay for in the normal course of your business, such as rent, telephone charges and broadband. You will need to keep a strict and detailed accounting of everything, from your phone bill to your pens. Everything that you touch in the normal course of your day is a cost of doing business and needs to be counted as an overhead. Items are all too often overlooked for the VAs that work from home. Just because you use something for home purposes does not mean that it is not an overhead cost. If you use it for your business, count it as an overhead cost. If you are in doubt, talk to your accountant about what you costs you should count as overhead.

Profit

Put simply; profit is what you have left over when you take what you are able to charge and subtract your overhead costs. As a business owner, your goal will be to increase your profit. You can do this by either increasing your billing or by decreasing your overhead. Ideally, you could do both. We could have a whole separate book on how to do those. I would suggest reviewing chapters 2, 3 and 4 if you need to increase your billing.

Tracking your time for billing

If you intend to bill on an hourly basis, you will need to be sure you are keeping an accurate account of the time you are spending on each client's work. You may well find you are working for several clients throughout the day, so you need to be certain that you are billing correctly for each.

It is common practice to use five-minute increments to work out your bill for the client. You may want to have an Excel spreadsheet open for tracking which clients you are working with and the time that you start and end working for each throughout the day. There are a number of other software packages that you can get for free from the internet, or you can purchase an application (app). I personally use Asana, and when I am at a client's site, I use an app on my phone to keep time. There are many others, so you will need to find the product and method of timekeeping that works for you. One of the VAs I employ prefers to write everything down on a daily calendar sheet I created for a Time Management seminar I ran.

Invoicing

It is best to invoice your clients on a monthly basis. You should include:

- Your name, business name and business address
- Client's name, business name and business address
- Details of the nature of the work undertaken
- Breakdown of hours spent on each task (or list of projects undertaken)
- Cost next to each task or project
- Details of any ancillary costs as referred to previously: postage, adverts, travel, for example
- Total invoice amount

It is also a good idea to include some simple terms and conditions for your services on your invoice. For example, you want to ensure that your client's payment is prompt and so should include 'Payment to be made within ten working days' as one of your conditions. Another point to include is your preferred method for payment; do you want a cheque or payment direct to your bank account? You should also state that any ancillary costs, as mentioned previously, will be itemised and that payment for these should be made alongside the basic hourly/project fees.

The type of terms and conditions you include may depend on the type of work you are undertaking. For example, if you are undertaking any design work, you may want to state that the design is your property until payment has been made for such.

Credit Control

Credit control policies are common throughout big businesses, and they refer to the terms of payment expected from a customer. Credit control for a VA or other small business is essential, and it is prudent to ensure that your clients understand and agree to the terms of your credit control policy prior to your beginning work for them. Enforcing the policy could be difficult for a small business – often big businesses employ people in a dedicated credit control role – but you need to be adamant about your payment terms and, if the worst comes to the worst, you do have the option of taking a client to a small claims court if they refuse to pay you. This should always be a last resort, and it is worth bearing in mind that you would need to prove to the court the work that was undertaken and the terms of the original agreement. This is where detailed record keeping comes into its own.

This is not meant to scare you off. You just need to know that you do have options but you do also need to be aware that it is possible you may not win the case, in which situation you would have to pay your fees (though these should be minimal).

Accounting Terms and Definitions

It may be helpful to get a general idea of some of the accounting terminology you will come across in running a business.

Accounting Period – Also known as the trading year, this is the period of time over which accounts are prepared for a business and is generally twelve months. Some businesses work with a standard calendar year of January to December while others fall in line with the taxation system of April through to the end of the following March.

Accrual Accounting – Accounting records are managed on the basis of all monies owed to the business and owned by the business at a given time, whether or not all payments have actually been received or paid out. For example, you are purchasing a new IT system, and the money has not yet left your account, but payment has been authorised so this will be recorded as an outgoing. At the same time, you are working on a large job for a client and have invoiced them but not yet received their payment – the amount due will also be taken into account in your financial records though it has not yet reached your bank account.

Break Even – The business is neither making a profit or a loss, but income is covering expenditure.

Bank Reconciliation – Matching accounting records to bank statements to ensure that records are correct and none are outstanding.

Cash Accounting – Finances are recorded as and when they happen, i.e. income is recorded only when payment is made into the company, and expenditure only when it actually occurs. Taking the example used for Accrual Accounting above, the payment for the IT equipment would show as an outgoing only when the money has left the account, and the income for the job you are working on will not register until payment for it is actually received.

Cash Flow – Simple day-to-day accounting of income received (sales made, invoices paid, for example.) and outgoings made (e.g. bills paid, purchases made) by the business.

Credit Control – Process and procedures used to ensure that payment is made as agreed.

Debtor Days – The average time it takes for payment to be made for services or goods sold. Useful for reviewing business and also planning ahead for accounting/forecasting purposes.

Depreciation – The value of a business asset decreases over time. For example, a computer becomes less valuable due to wear and tear and, as advances in technology are made, your once state-of-the-art IT system becomes dated. In financial terms, depreciating an asset is a way of writing off the cost of an item over the term of its useful life, rather than in one lump sum. This is done for tax and accounting reasons. For example, the cost of your computer may be accounted for in monthly sums over three years – this can be charged against earnings as a legitimate cost of your business. This is definitely something which you should discuss with your accountant if you wish to explore the advantages/disadvantages for your own business.

Gross Margin – Business sales/income minus the direct cost of the goods or services sold but not taking into account operating costs, overheads or taxes.

Net Margin – Business income minus all deductions such as direct costs, operating costs and overheads but usually before the deduction of taxes.

Nominal Codes/General Ledger Codes – Used to identify particular aspects of a business's accounts; rather than using a specific name, e.g. 'Marketing Work', a code will be used. The detail for each nominal code will include income and outgoings related to that aspect of the business's finances.

Operating Costs – These costs are broken down into two sections, Variable Costs and Fixed Costs. Variable Costs are costs that can change during the running of your business for example Networking costs. Fixed Costs are costs that will not change if you are doing business or not, for example, Rent, Broadband,

Pre-Payment – Payment made before it is due, e.g. your client pays you in advance for work you are going to undertake. This would be extremely useful if your work for them involves an amount of expense, for example ordering marketing material.

Pricing –Mark-up and Margin

Markup – Creating a profit for your business by selling on an item or service with a percentage added onto the price you paid for it. For example, if you outsource a piece of work on behalf of a client and pay £200 for it, you could mark it up by ten percent and charge your client £220.

Margin – This is the percentage of the sale price which is profit. If you have outsourced a piece of work and paid £200 for it, and charged your client £220, your margin is not the 10% by which you have marked up from the price at which you bought, but 9.1% as £20 is around 9.1% of the £220 you sold.

Profit & Loss (P&L) – Accounting method usually tracked monthly, showing a company's performance and taking into account income and expenditure such as operating expenses and depreciation amounts for that period. The budget amount for that period is often used in a P&L to review a business's performance against the allowances planned.

Provisions – Expected expenses such as bad debt can be taken into account (made provision for) in the current business accounts, before the expense actually occurs, which reduces the current company profit in the period within which the provision is made. This can be useful if you are having an exceptionally good year and are able to take the hit from this provision without eroding your profits by too much. This is something which you should discuss with your accountant.

Stock – Raw Materials, Work in Progress and Finished Goods

Raw Materials – Items bought by a business often for manufacture or development - raw materials are items prior to any work being done on them. An example of raw materials for a VA may be a stock of plain paper, which will be used for printing business letterheads and in turn, business correspondence.

Work in Progress – Items which are in progress but not yet finished – using the example above, the paper has had the letterheads printed on it but has not yet been used for specific printing such as correspondence or marketing literature.

Finished Goods – The items bought as raw materials are through the production process. The example we are using would see the plain paper (raw materials) having been printed with company letterhead and other details (work in progress), then specific text such as marketing information or correspondence as requested by your client (finished goods).

Write-Offs – When an asset is of no future use to a business, its value can be 'written off', i.e. recorded as an expense in one period. For example, the computer which has been depreciating over three years breaks after two years. At this point, its remaining value is recorded as an expense, rather than continuing through to the end of its depreciation period.

Financial Reports and Statements

Trial Balance – Statement of accounts which show whether the amount debited from accounts equals those credited.

Balance Sheet – An up-to-date, detailed record of incomings and outgoings for a business, which will show on one side where money has come from (invoices, loans, for example.) and on the other where it has gone to (e.g. purchases made and bills paid). Both sides must always balance.

Budget – Financial planning for an amount of time (often the financial year) will involve determining your budget for the year and how it will break down to different types of expense. Using forecasting where possible will help you work this out, and identifying any necessary costs such as professional membership, upgrades of equipment, website hosting, for example. By employing a budget, you should be able to manage the business finances confidently. However you should also be aware that there will almost always be unforeseen expenses (and hopefully income as well.), so it is best to err on the side of caution and allow some leeway rather than think that you can know everything in advance.

Cash Flow Statement – Financial statement which shows the incoming and outgoing of cash through a business and is a useful tool for showing a company's financial standing in the short term.

Forecast – Forecasting is used to try and predict a business's finances over a following period, whether a month, quarter or a year. Past costs and sales can be used, as well as any external factors. For example, one of your clients may have used you reliably for the last three years, and their company may be expanding and requiring your services more (or perhaps less if they have grown enough to take on their own assistant). This kind of knowledge can help you with your internal forecasting.

Management Accounting – Generally for internal company use, management accounting is designed for use by managers within an organisation, to enable them to analyse current and past financial records. Taking into account this information, they are able to plan and make effective decisions which will, in turn, affect the business's future finances.

Legal Status of Your Business

What is your business going to be?

If you are unsure about which type of business structure you would like to create, then it is imperative that you speak to a solicitor or an accountant. It is vital that you fully understand ALL of the repercussions of owning a business. You need to understand which business structure will work best for you and your lifestyle.

It is also a good idea to think ahead about what you want to do with your business after you have set it up. Do you want to set your business so that you can sell it at a later date or do you want to earn some money to ensure that your bills are paid, and your family is taken care of and you cover all your expenses? There are no right or wrong answers here. The business you set up must work for you and your family.

Your Attitude Towards Risk

Your personal attitude towards risk should have some bearing on the type of business you choose to create.

Personally, I am not a very good risk taker; for example, when I go into an amusement arcade, I set myself a limit of £1 to spend and make sure that I find all the 2p machines to use. My mortgage is also a fixed rate repayment mortgage. I know it is more expensive in the long run, but I need to know what my outgoings are each month and how much spare money I have at the end of each month that can be used on other things.

However, despite not being keen on taking risks, this never put me off running my own business. I just never felt that setting up, running and owning a business is much of a risk. It was something I always knew I was going to do; I knew I would be good at it. I knew that I would have to work hard and put in many hours. I just didn't know what this business was going to be.

Nevertheless, I had a house and all the costs associated with it, as well as other general expenses that I needed to take care of each month. I took the view that if my business did for some reason fail, which I was sure it wouldn't (but 'just in case'), I would still need somewhere to live, I would still need money to take care of my general expenses, and I don't want to live with debt. It was for this reason that I chose to set up as a Limited Company. I later changed my businesses legal status to a Limited Liability Partnership as there was a change in tax law and there were tax advantages for me to make this change.

There are some costs involved in being a Limited Company and a Limited Liability Partnership. Every year I have to pay £30 to the Companies House to tell them I am still trading (this is £15 if I register online). I have to pay my accountant each year to create my accounts, which need to be submitted to the Companies House annually. I have accepted that these additional costs are going to be about £600 each year, but it suits my lifestyle and my aversion to risk.

Having said all of the above, I have found that running a Virtual Assistant business does not need much expenditure. If you are careful, know what you are doing and plan appropriately, you should never find yourself in a position where you have any debt.

Below is a description of the types of business you can set up and a list of advantages and disadvantages for each.

A Sole Trader

A sole trader is someone who chooses to set up their business on their own, and more importantly, they own the business outright. An example of a sole trader is a plumber, electrician or consultant; some virtual assistants also choose to start their business as a sole trader. It is the simplest and quickest way of starting up your business. If you start your business as a sole trader, you do have the option to change your company's legal structure to a limited company, a limited liability partnership or a partnership at a later date. As a sole trader, you will need to register your employment status as self-employed with HM Revenue and Customs.

It is vitally important to remember that as a sole trader you will be personally liable for any debts that are created when running your business. This means that if you incur any business debts, you could lose your home if you are unable to pay them.

The first step to becoming a sole trader is to choose a business name. You can trade under your own name or come up with a suitable business name. If you do decide to use a business name, you must ensure that all your business stationery and corporate communications display the trading name of the business along with your own name.

You should check that your trading name is not the same or too similar to that of another business that already exists to avoid confusion and legal problems.

A Sole Trader - Advantages

- Easy to set up; limited paperwork to be maintained
- The cheapest way to start a business
- You keep all the profits (after paying all relevant taxes)
- Accounting and financial record keeping is very simple
- National Insurance (NI) is low
- You keep your independence
- You can take on staff

A Sole Trader - Disadvantages

- Any business debts from your own income, savings or assets
- Lack of support — everything is down to you
- More difficult to raise capital to finance the business
- It is harder to sell the business or to pass it on
- Employing staff can be expensive to the business, and you will be responsible for ensuring they pay the correct Income Tax and NI. Also, as an employer, you will also need to pay Employer's NI. This will mean that you will have to set up a Pay As You Earn (PAYE) payroll system. You, as the employer, will be responsible for ensuring that this is done and that the government is properly paid.

Partnership

There are two types of Partnerships that I will discuss here: an Ordinary Partnership and a Limited Liability Partnership

An **Ordinary Partnership** can be set up when two or more people choose to run a business together. Each partner will be self-employed and will take a share of the profit, the decision-making process, and the debts.

A Partnership has no legal existence distinct from the partners themselves. If one of the partners resigns, dies or goes bankrupt, the partnership must be dissolved - although the business can still continue.'

Ordinary Partnership Advantages

- Raise more capital by introducing more partners.
- You can have 'sleeping partners' to help raise money but who don't get involved in running the business on a day-to-day basis (this will depend on your Partnership agreement).
- The risk of setting up a business is shared.
- Each partner takes a share of the profits.
- This is a simple and flexible way of setting up a business.

Ordinary Partnership Disadvantages

- Each partner will be personally liable for all of the business debt, even if the debt was caused by another partner.
- You need to find someone you trust to go into business with and ensure you have a partnership contract.

A friend of mine (we'll call her Victoria) set up a partnership business with her best friend. They had been friends since meeting at school when they were five years old. In their early 20s, they decided to set up and run livery stables together as they were both passionate about horses and knew how to run a yard.

The partnership was a verbal partnership with no clear boundaries on who was to do what and when. It ran very well for a number of years, and the yard gained a reputation as being one of the best in the area. There was even a waiting list of horse owners who wanted to join the yard.

Victoria's friend eventually married and even though her new husband had nothing to do with the partnership, he started to make suggestions as to how to grow the business. Without Victoria knowing, her friend started a marketing campaign to promote the yard. The marketing campaign was marginally successful, but as they already had a waiting list of clients, it was a worthless exercise. It also, more importantly for Victoria, incurred a number of costs for the business. As this was a partnership business, Victoria was of course personally liable for these debts alongside her friend.

Victoria went to work on a Monday to find that her friend was nowhere to be seen. She spent a week worrying about her friend and a further two weeks of investigation to ensure that her friend was OK and nothing had happened to her. Her friend would not answer her phone, no one was at home when Victoria called around, and her friend's parents would not tell Victoria anything.

Eventually, Victoria found herself on her own looking after the livery yard and responsible for over £35,000 worth of debt. Her friend decided that she couldn't cope with the mounting debt (Victoria had known nothing about) and the responsibilities of running a business which had been very successful until the new ideas on how to improve the business had been undertaken.

Victoria was forced to close the yard as she couldn't physically run the business on her own. To close the business took about six months and Victoria was forced to work seven days a week from 7am to 8pm. It took her almost ten years to pay off this debt as her friend refused to accept any responsibility.

Victoria should have had a legal agreement setting up the rules and responsibilities of the partnership. There were no boundaries set within this business, and as a result, it failed.

A **Limited Liability Partnership** (LLP) is very similar in trading status to a limited company and an ordinary partnership 'in that a number of individuals or limited companies share in the risks, costs, responsibilities and profits of the business.'

The major difference is that any liability is limited to the amount of money you have invested in the business, as well as any possible personal guarantees you have made to raise finance.

If you decide that an LLP is the right choice for you, make sure that all members of the business partnership have a members' legal agreement drawn up, exactly as you would with an ordinary partnership. It is vital that you understand the ground rules in your partnership. Who will be in charge of sales, how the profits will be divided, what sort of items can you claim in expenses, for example. You need to ensure that everyone is clear about their roles and responsibilities.

Limited liability partnership – Advantages

- The members of an LLP are limited for losses or debts in a similar way to limited companies
- It has the flexibility of a partnership
- It is taxed on profits rather than on drawings, the money you take out of the business.

Limited liability partnership - Disadvantages

- You need to file annual accounts
- You must register at Companies House and send a copy of your yearly accounts (there is a small fee for this)
- At least one director, who must be over 16 years of age
- Self-assessment returns to HM Revenue and Customs
- You need to have a minimum of two members within the partnership to set up an LLP

Limited Company

A Limited Company is a separate entity from its owners. This means that the company's finances are separate from the owner's personal finances. A Limited Company is a legal entity (sometimes it is easier to think of it as a person with their own rights) and is liable for any debts. The legal protection given to owners of limited companies can outweigh the initial costs and ongoing running costs of setting up a limited company.

If you began your business as a sole trader, and your business expands, you may want to develop your image and change your trading style to that of a limited company.

Limited Company - Advantages

- More credibility to the business
- Easier to raise capital as you can sell shares in your business
- It is easier to sell a business as a limited company
- Liability is limited to the amount you have invested in the company, rather than any debts that are incurred from trading
- Tax advantages, high earners, keeping money in the business
- Offer business continuity when owners sell or retire

Limited Company - Disadvantages

- Annual accounts can be more complicated to produce
- National Insurance payments are higher because you have to pay employer's and employee's National Insurance contributions for staff and directors
- If your turnover reaches over £56m, you will have to have an independent audit — another business cost
- As members of the board of directors running a company, you are accountable to your shareholders
- If shareholders invest in the business, there is a risk that they could lose, instead of make, money.

Setting up your business structure is very important to ensure that your business complies with the various legal rules and regulations within the United Kingdom.

Remember all the key points relating to the financial and accounting side of your business.

If you are worried about the legal status of your business, speak to your solicitor or your accountant to get their advice. This book is designed as a guide and is based on my experience only. I have often called my accountant for his help and support.

No matter how long you have been in business or what you know, the legal, financial and status of your business will change and getting up-to-the-minute advice and support for the professional is always advisable.

Section Five
Conclusion

In conclusion, I would like to say that I have run my Virtual Assistant business since 2002. It has been one of the best career decisions I have ever made. I thoroughly enjoy meeting my clients and deciding whom I will and won't work with and the tasks I will take. It has taken a long time to get to this stage. At the beginning of my business, I took every job I could for the income. Now I have become more selective and fire clients I don't want to work with anymore.

Since 2002 I have discovered that there are many differences to running different businesses. I have learnt how a sculpture is made in bronze, resin and a combination of the two, I have learnt how to prepare for a speech in front of 2000 people, I have learnt how to organise a membership networking group and how to run a plumbing business. What I have also learnt is that each business owner has their strengths and weaknesses and it has been one of my roles and honour to help support the weaknesses.

I have also learnt how my business works, what my strengths are and where I needed to learn more. I have learnt how to employ staff and how to look after my business.

I love this industry, and I hope that you will love it as much as I do. You can never guarantee what you will be doing from one day to the next; you can never guarantee who will walk into your office and ask for help and support.

I would like to wish you good luck in running your Virtual Assistant business, and I hope that you will enjoy running your business as much as I have enjoyed your business.

www.ingramcontent.com/pod-product-compliance
Lightning Source LLC
Chambersburg PA
CBHW060628210326
41520CB00010B/1523